U.S. Department of Justice
Office of Justice Programs
National Institute of Justice

JUNE 09

NIJ

Special REPORT

Practical Implications of Current Domestic Violence Research: For Law Enforcement, Prosecutors and Judges

www.ojp.usdoj.gov/nij

U.S. Department of Justice
Office of Justice Programs
810 Seventh Street N.W.
Washington, DC 20531

Eric H. Holder, Jr.
Attorney General

Laurie O. Robinson
Acting Assistant Attorney General

Kristina Rose
Acting Director, National Institute of Justice

This and other publications and products of the National Institute of Justice can be found at:

National Institute of Justice
www.ojp.usdoj.gov/nij

Office of Justice Programs
Innovation • Partnerships • Safer Neighborhoods
www.ojp.usdoj.gov

JUNE 09

Practical Implications of Current Domestic Violence Research: For Law Enforcement, Prosecutors and Judges

Andrew R. Klein

NCJ 225722

Kristina Rose
Acting Director, National Institute of Justice

This NIJ e-pub is based on three final reports submitted to the National Institute of Justice under contract number 2007M-07032, which was awarded to Advocates for Human Potential.

Findings and conclusions of the research reported here are those of the author and do not necessarily reflect the official position or policies of the U.S. Department of Justice.

This document is not intended to create, does not create, and may not be relied upon to create any rights, substantive or procedural, enforceable at law by any party in any matter civil or criminal.

The National Institute of Justice is a component of the Office of Justice Programs, which also includes the Bureau of Justice Assistance; the Bureau of Justice Statistics; the Community Capacity Development Office; the Office for Victims of Crime; the Office of Juvenile Justice and Delinquency Prevention; and the Office of Sex Offender Sentencing, Monitoring, Apprehending, Registering, and Tracking (SMART).

 SPECIAL REPORT / JUNE 09

Contents

Preface vi
    Performance Measures.. vi

1. Overview of Domestic Violence... 1
    1.1   How widespread is nonfatal domestic violence?... 1
    1.2   What percentage of calls to police are to report domestic violence?................... 1
    1.3   What time of day does domestic violence occur? 2
    1.4   How widespread is stalking? 2
    1.5   How widespread are sexual assaults of intimate partners? 2
    1.6   How widespread is fatal domestic violence?... 3
    1.7   How widespread are multiple forms of domestic violence against the same victims? 4

2. Reporting and Arrests 5
    2.1   To what extent is domestic violence reported to law enforcement and what percentage actually reaches the courts? 5
    2.2   At what point do victims report domestic violence?... 6
    2.3   Which victims are likely to report domestic violence? 7
    2.4   Does the quality of the law enforcement response influence whether domestic violence is reported? 7
    2.5   Who else reports domestic violence? 8
    2.6   Are there other major sources for reports of domestic violence? 8
    2.7   What kinds of domestic violence are reported to law enforcement and are prosecuted? 9
    2.8   Do arrest rates correspond to actual rates of domestic violence and stalking based on victim surveys? 10
    2.9   Do stalking arrests correspond to actual stalking rates as reported by victims? 11
    2.10   Is arrest the best response? 11
    2.11   What should law enforcement"s response be if the suspect is gone when they arrive? 12
    2.12   Who is the primary/predominant aggressor? 13

3. Perpetrator Characteristics 15
    3.1   What is their gender? 15
    3.2   What age are they? 16
    3.3   Are they likely to be known to law enforcement already?................................ 16
    3.4   Are they likely to be drug and/or alcohol abusers? 17
    3.5   Are they likely to be mentally ill or have certain personality traits?................ 18
    3.6   Do abusers stick with one victim?.. 18
    3.7   How many abusers are likely to do it again?... 19
    3.8   Are abusers at risk for committing new nondomestic violence crimes?.......... 20
    3.9   When are abusers likely to reabuse?.. 21
    3.10   Which abusers are likely to do it again in the short term? 22
    3.11   Is gender an important risk factor? 22
    3.12   Is age an important risk factor? 22
    3.13   Is prior arrest history an important risk factor?.. 22
    3.14   Is substance abuse an important risk factor?... 23

3.15 Are victims accurate predictors of reabuse? 24
3.16 Are there other common risk factors associated with reabuse? 25
3.17 What factors are not associated with reabuse? 25
3.18 Do the widely used risk instruments accurately predict reabuse? 26
3.19 Which abusers are most likely to try to kill their victims? 26
3.20 How critical is the presence of firearms and other weapons? 26
3.21 What are other lethality risk markers? 27
3.22 What are the risk markers for severe injury? 28

4. Victim Characteristics 29
    4.1 Are victim characteristics and actions important factors in assessing the likelihood of abuse? 29
    4.2 To what extent do victims engage in alcohol and drug abuse? 29
    4.3 Why do some victims behave as they do? 30
    4.4 Do male domestic violence victims differ from female victims? 31

5. Law Enforcement Responses 33
    5.1 Are specialized law enforcement domestic violence units effective in responding to domestic violence? 33
    5.2 Do they influence prosecutions and convictions of abuse suspects? 33
    5.3 Do they influence victim behavior? 33
    5.4 Do they reduce reabuse? 33
    5.5 Do they increase victim satisfaction? 34
    5.6 Should law enforcement agencies participate in coordinated community responses? 34
    5.7 Does domestic violence training improve law enforcement responses to victims? 35

6. Prosecution Responses 36
    6.1 What is the current level of domestic violence prosecution across the country? 36
    6.2 Can most domestic violence arrest cases be successfully prosecuted in court? 36
    6.3 Will aggressive prosecutions or sentences increase the demand for trials? ... 38
    6.4 Do victims want their abusers prosecuted? 38
    6.5 Why do a minority of victims oppose prosecution? 39
    6.6 Is victim fear of prosecution well founded? 40
    6.7 Can prosecutors increase victim cooperation? 40
    6.8 Should prosecutors follow victim preferences when prosecuting offenders? .. 42
    6.9 What evidence is typically available to prosecute domestic violence cases? . 42
    6.10 Can cases be successfully prosecuted without the victim? 43
    6.11 Can successful prosecutions be increased? 45
    6.12 What does adoption of no-drop policies actually mean? 45
    6.13 What kind of dispositions do most suspects receive? 45
    6.14 Does prosecuting domestic violence offenders deter reabuse? 46
    6.15 When does sentencing of domestic violence defendants not necessarily prevent reabuse? 48
    6.16 Are defendants who don't show up in court more at risk for reabusing than those who do? 48
    6.17 Can "first" offenders be safely diverted or discharged? 48
    6.18 Do specialized prosecution units work? 49

    6.19 What characterizes specialized prosecution units? 50

7. Judicial Responses 52
    7.1   Does sentencing domestic violence offenders deter reabuse? 52
    7.2   Should judges follow victim preferences when determining sentences? 53
    7.3   What should the response be when the suspect is brought in on an arrest or
          court-default warrant? 53
    7.4   What are current abuser sentencing practices? 54
    7.5   What accounts for dispositions? 54
    7.6   Are defendants who don't show up in court more at risk for reabuse than
          those who do? 55
    7.7   Can "first" offenders be safely diverted or discharged? 55
    7.8   Who obtains civil protective orders? 56
    7.9   When and why do victims ask for orders? 56
    7.10 How many abusers violate court protective orders? 57
    7.11 Do protective orders work? 58
    7.12 Does judicial demeanor make a difference? 59
    7.13 Do specialized domestic violence courts work? 60
    7.14 What makes specialized domestic violence courts different? 61
    7.15 Do enhanced domestic violence dispositions require enhanced
          postdisposition court time and resources? 63
    7.16 Does the type of postdispositional monitoring matter? 63
    7.17 Does probation supervision of abusers reduce likelihood of reabuse? 64

8. Intervention Programs 65
    8.1   Do batterer intervention programs prevent reabuse? 65
    8.2   Does the type or length of batterer intervention program make a difference? 65
    8.3   Do couples counseling or anger management treatment programs prevent
          reabuse? 66
    8.4   Does alcohol and drug treatment prevent reabuse? 67
    8.5   Are court-referred batterers likely to complete batterer programs? 67
    8.6   Do those who complete batterer programs do better than those who fail? 68
    8.7   Can court monitoring enhance batterer intervention program attendance? 69
    8.8   Which batterers are likely to fail to attend mandated batterer intervention
          treatment? 70
    8.9   When are noncompliant abusers likely to drop out of batterer programs? 71
    8.10 What should the prosecutor"s response be if court-referred abusers are
          noncompliant with programs? 71
    8.11 What should the judge"s response be if court-referred abusers are
          noncompliant with programs? 72
    8.12 What should the prosecutor"s or judge"s response be to abusers who
          reoffend while enrolled or after completing a batterer intervention program? ... 73
    8.13 What effect do batterer intervention program referrals have on victims? 73

References 74

Preface

The purpose of this work is to describe to practitioners what the research tells us about domestic violence, including its perpetrators and victims, the impact of current responses to it and, more particularly, the implications of that research for day-to-day, real-world responses to domestic violence by law enforcement officers, prosecutors and judges.

Although many state and federal statutes define domestic violence broadly, for the purposes of this work, it is confined to offenses committed by and against current or former intimate partners, married or unmarried, with or without children.

Most but not all of the research reports discussed in this brief are from studies funded by the National Institute of Justice and/or published in a variety of refereed journals. For example, several studies of women seeking hospital emergency room treatment for injuries inflicted by intimate partners are included because, although of primary concern to the medical community, these studies underscore victim characteristics found in criminal-justice-related research, suggesting how representative the latter is.

Less rigorous research reports are also included because of the quality of their data collection or because they provide accurate examples of performance measures. For example, several performance evaluations of specific programs are included, not because they address program effectiveness in terms of preventing reabuse but because they provide concrete examples of what specific programs can achieve in terms of important program outputs such as arrest or successful prosecution rates. Some of the most extensive examinations of prosecution practices have been conducted by newspaper-initiated investigations in which reporters gained access to state court data tapes of thousands of cases.

Although some research findings may be questionable because researchers used less than rigorous research methodology, the research itself may be cited because it contains accurate data illustrating an important phenomenon. The data are unaffected by the research design used by the researchers. For example, although Jacobson and Gottman"s findings regarding the typology of batterers [128] have been questioned, their reported observations, if not their conclusions, have been confirmed. [158] They are cited in support of the proposition that batterer reaction to their violence is not uniform but are not cited in support of their more controversial conclusion that all batterers fall into two distinct categories.

The policy and practice implications are based on the evidence provided by the research and are therefore confined to areas specifically addressed by researchers. Consequently, the implications described in this brief do not constitute a comprehensive listing of promising practices or even policies and procedures widely recognized to be effective. Whenever possible, policy implications are based on multiple studies. However, in some instances, where only one study examined an issue deemed to be important to practitioners, policy implications may be drawn from just that one study. In such cases, the narrative will alert readers that the research has not yet been replicated.

Performance Measures

The performance measures (featured in textboxes) include examples of specific programs, specific jurisdictions" achievements, or surveys of multiple departments. These measures are included to provide examples of what a specific, real-life program or jurisdiction can accomplish.

Because jurisdictions vary, these measures may not be replicable in all other jurisdictions but suggest what may be achieved in similar jurisdictions.

NIJ SPECIAL REPORT / JUNE 09

1. Overview of Domestic Violence

1.1 How widespread is nonfatal domestic violence?

According to the latest 2005 National Crime Victimization Survey (NCVS), during the period from 1993 to 2005, the average annual domestic violence rate per 1,000 persons (age 12 or older) for intimate partners and/or relatives was 5.9 for females and 2.1 for males. About one-third of the victims reported they were physically attacked; two-thirds were threatened with attack or death. A little more than half (50.5 percent) of the female victims suffered an injury, but only 4.5 percent were seriously injured. Slightly more than 3 percent were sexually assaulted. Fewer male victims — 41.5 percent — reported injuries, of which less than 5 percent were serious injuries. Those males or females who were separated (or divorced) experienced more nonfatal domestic violence than those who were together. [27]

Victimization rates vary among different subpopulations. The highest reported rates are for Native American women. [154]

1.2 What percentage of calls to police are to report domestic violence?

Domestic-violence-related police calls have been found to constitute the single largest category of calls received by police, accounting for 15 to more than 50 percent of all calls. [68, 114] Not all domestic violence calls are for activities that constitute crimes. Several New York studies, for example, found that 65 percent of such calls in upstate New York pertained to criminal conduct. In New York City, the police department found that 35 percent of reports pertained to specific chargeable index or other criminal offenses. [165, 184] In San Diego, approximately 25 percent of calls for service in domestic violence cases result in an arrest. [196]

Implications for Law Enforcement

Given the large numbers adversely affected by domestic violence and that victims" prime countermeasure — leaving their abusers — may not stop the abuse, law enforcement agencies must commit time, resources and attention to domestic violence as they do to confront any other major crime. For this reason, all law enforcement agencies should have a domestic violence policy that specifies, at a minimum, that written reports be completed on all domestic violence calls and, if no arrest is made, the reports fully explain the circumstances why not. (Research basis: Disparate national surveys, supplemented by local police department studies.)

> **Performance Measure:** A total of 77 percent of police departments have written operational procedures for responding to emergency domestic violence calls, and larger departments are most likely to have such written procedures. Most procedures include requiring the dispatcher to ask about weapons, check for protection orders, and advise the caller to stay on the line until police arrive. [213] (Research basis: Representative sample of 368 drawn from 14,000 law enforcement agencies across the nation.)

Implications for Prosecutors and Judges

Given the large numbers adversely affected by domestic violence and that victims" prime countermeasure — leaving their abusers — may not stop the abuse, and given the amount of time committed to responding to domestic violence calls and arresting and prosecuting alleged offenders, prosecutors and judges must commit sufficient resources and attention to ensure that domestic violence cases are handled efficiently and effectively. (Research basis: Disparate national surveys, supplemented by local police department and prosecution studies.)

1.3 What time of day does domestic violence occur?

According to the NCVS, most offenses (60 percent) occur between 6 p.m. and 6 a.m. at the victim"s home. [27]

Implications for Law Enforcement

Although all potential responding law enforcement officers must be trained and prepared to deal with domestic violence, if the agency has only a limited number of victim advocates, related auxiliary personnel, or volunteers to assist on domestic violence calls, priority should be given to the 6 p.m. to 6 a.m. time period. (Research basis: National survey data from 1993 to 2004.)

1.4 How widespread is stalking?

Estimates of stalking vary, depending upon how it is defined. A 1995-1996 National Violence Against Women Survey (NVAWS) found that 5 per 1,000 females (18 and older) and 2 per 1,000 males report being stalked annually, using a conservative definition that requires victims to suffer a high level of fear. Eighty percent of stalking victims are women, and 87 percent of stalkers are male. Women were stalked by spouses or ex-spouses (38 percent), current or former intimates (10 percent), dating partners (14 percent), other relatives (4 percent), acquaintances (19 percent), and strangers (23 percent). The percentages add to more than 100 percent because some women reported being stalked by more than one person. Males were more likely than females to be stalked by strangers (36 percent) and acquaintances (34 percent). [131, 207] Furthermore, research suggests a close association between stalking and murders of women by intimate partners. One study, for example, found more than half (54 percent) of female intimate partner murder victims had reported stalking to police prior to their murders by the stalkers. [156]

Implications for Law Enforcement

It is important for law enforcement officers to correctly identify stalking behavior in order to accurately analyze victim risk and to use stalking laws appropriately. Even if the stalker is not charged, stalking constitutes a red flag for potential lethality. (Research basis: National study of 141 murders and 65 attempted murders of women, and confirmation in other stalking studies.)

Implications for Prosecutors and Judges

Whether stalkers are specifically charged or not, it is important for prosecutors and judges to correctly identify stalking behavior and recognize its significance in order to give victims maximum protection against potentially lethal abusers. (Research basis: National study of 141 murders and 65 attempted murders of women, and confirmation in other stalking studies.)

1.5 How widespread are sexual assaults of intimate partners?

If there is physical abuse in domestic violence, studies suggest that there is probably sexual abuse as well. A Texas study found that almost 70 percent of women seeking protective orders were raped, most (79 percent) repeatedly. [157] Although reporting a lower rate, an earlier Massachusetts study found 55 percent of female restraining order petitioners reported to interviewers that they had been sexually assaulted by their abusers, although **no one** had included this in her affidavit requesting a protective order. [143] Female victims similarly underreported sexual abuse in a Colorado study. Although 20 to 50 percent of women seeking protective orders had been subjected to a variety of abuse, including forced sex within the preceding year, only 4 percent listed forced sex on the complaint form requesting the temporary restraining order. [105]

Implications for Law Enforcement

Investigators should be alert to possible sexual as well as physical abuse in interviewing or investigating domestic assaults. Judgment must be used as to how and when to approach potential victims of sexual assaults. (Research basis: National survey as well as disparate individual studies from multiple regions.)

Implications for Prosecutors and Judges

Prosecutors should be aware that sexual abuse is often part of domestic violence, although victims may not report it or be prepared to cooperate in its prosecution. Even if prosecutors cannot file or prosecute, evidence of sexual assaults should be taken into account when prosecutors and judges consider abuser risk and victim vulnerability in terms of filing other charges and making appropriate sentencing recommendations, bail decisions, issuing protective orders, and sentencing abusers after pleas or convictions. (Research basis: National survey as well as disparate individual studies from multiple regions.)

1.6 How widespread is fatal domestic violence?

According to the Supplementary Homicide Reports of the FBI's Uniform Crime Reporting Program in 2005, 1,181 females and 329 males were killed by their intimate partners. [27] The number of men killed has dropped by almost three-quarters since 1976, whereas the number of women killed has only dropped by a quarter. The number of white females killed has declined the least — only 6 percent. Intimate partner homicides constituted 11 percent of all homicides between 1976 and 2005, 30 percent of all female murders (1976-2004), and 3 percent of all male murders (1976-2005). The proportion of female homicide victims killed by an intimate partner is increasing. Unlike nonfatal domestic violence, most intimate partner homicides (54 percent) involve spouses or ex-spouses, although intimate partner homicides for unmarried couples are approaching the rate for married or divorced couples.

Intimate partner homicides may also involve third parties, including children, bystanders, employers and lawyers, among others. For example, according to the Washington State Domestic Violence Fatality Review, between 1997 and 2004, there were 313 domestic violence fatality cases in that state involving 416 homicides, including 23 children, 32 friends/family members of primary intimate partner victims, 19 new boyfriends of primary intimate victims, one co-worker of the primary intimate victim, three law enforcement officers responding to the intimate partner homicide, 9 abusers killed by law enforcement, and 10 abusers killed by a friend or family member of victims. Additionally, 93 abusers committed suicide after killing their victim(s). [199]

Implications for Law Enforcement

To reduce female homicides generally, law enforcement must give priority to the protection of female intimate partners. (Research basis: National data collected by the Federal Bureau of Investigation.)

Implications for Prosecutors and Judges

To reduce female homicides generally, prosecutors and judges must give priority to the protection of female intimates. Reduction of female intimate homicides will also reduce collateral homicides of children, other family members, and responding law enforcement officers as well as reducing abuser suicides. (Research basis: National data collected by the Federal Bureau of Investigation, and multiple state and local fatality reviews.)

1.7 How widespread are multiple forms of domestic violence against the same victims?

Analysis of NVAWS data revealed that 18 percent of the women who experienced abuse experienced **systemic abuse**, meaning they were likely to suffer physical attacks (with and without weapons) and strangulation; of these women, 24.4 percent also experienced sexual assault, and 47.8 percent experienced stalking. [153] A study of dating violence similarly found substantial overlap between physical and sexual victimization. [222]

Implications for Law Enforcement

A full investigation may indicate additional, even more serious incidents of domestic violence than the one to which the law enforcement officers respond. (Research basis: A national survey and a five-year longitudinal study of college students from schools considered representative of state colleges attended by 80 percent of all U.S. college students.)

Implications for Prosecutors

A post-arrest investigation by the prosecutor may indicate additional, even more serious incidents of domestic violence than the one specifically noted by law enforcement officers. Rarely does the reported abuse incident represent a single isolated, atypical act. Appropriate charges should be filed that cover the range of criminal behaviors of abusers. In light of the United State"s Supreme Court case, *Crawford* v. *Washington*, 541 U.S. 36 (2004), and its increased demand for live victim testimony, prosecutors must work with law enforcement to uncover any evidence of abuser intimidation of victims that would inhibit the victim"s testimony. Such evidence may also be used in preparing victim impact statements. (Research basis: A national survey and a five-year longitudinal study of college students from schools considered representative of state colleges attended by 80 percent of all U.S. college students.)

Implications for Judges

Although called upon to respond to discrete criminal charges, judges must insist that they receive sufficient information to reveal any pattern of systemic, abusive behaviors in order to accurately understand the victim"s vulnerability. (Research basis: A national survey and a five-year longitudinal study of college students from schools considered representative of state colleges attended by 80 percent of all U.S. college students.)

2. Reporting and Arrests

2.1 To what extent is domestic violence reported to law enforcement and what percentage actually reaches the courts?

As with any crime, not all incidents of domestic violence are reported to law enforcement, not all incidents reported to law enforcement are forwarded to prosecutors, and even fewer are prosecuted.

Both the older NVAWS and the more contemporary NCVS reports agree that victims do not report all cases of their victimization to police. According to the NVAWS, only 27 percent of women and 13.5 percent of men who were physically assaulted by an intimate partner reported their assault to law enforcement. Less than 20 percent of women victims reported intimate partner rapes to police. Reporting rates for stalking were higher, with 52 percent of women and 36 percent of men reporting stalking incidents to law enforcement. A succession of NCVS surveys over the past several decades find much higher reporting rates (but for far fewer victimizations). According to these surveys, reporting to police of nonfatal partner victimization has increased for all victims (male and female) to more than 62 percent, with no gap between male and female victim reporting rates. The highest reporting rate is for black females (70.2 percent) and the lowest is for black males (46.5 percent). [27]

Comparing hundreds of police domestic violence incident reports with victim statements at four sites in three different states, researchers found that a proportion of victims deny abuse documented by police. Researchers found 29 percent of victims reported "no assault," contradicting police findings. Ironically, their alleged assailants were more likely to admit to the assaults, with only 19 percent reporting "no assault." However, suspects were more likely than victims to minimize the severity of the assaults. [63] Researchers also found that some victims do not report repeated incidents of abuse to police. A review of NCVS data from 1992 through 2002 found that, although 60 percent of the victims had been assaulted by their intimate partners before, only half of the latest survey assaults were reported to police, and these included reports made by persons other than the victim. Prior unreported domestic violence may be more serious than the incident actually reported. [63]

Reasons given in the 2005 NCVS for not reporting abuse incidents included a belief that the abuse was a private or personal matter (22 percent for females, 39 percent for males), fear of reprisal (12 percent for females, 5 percent for males), a desire to protect the suspect (14 percent for females, 16 percent for males), and a belief that police won't do anything (8 percent for females and for males). [27, 63]

Once reported, police arrest rates vary, depending on the jurisdiction and how each defines domestic violence. Arrests for domestic violence per 1,000 persons ranged from 3.2 in Omaha, Neb. (2003), to 12.2 in Wichita, Kan. (2000). [135]

Prosecution rates similarly vary. A review of 26 domestic violence prosecution studies from across the country found prosecutions per arrest ranged from 4.6 percent in Milwaukee in 1992 to 94 percent reported in Hamilton, Ohio, in 2005. The average rate was 63.8 percent, and the median rate was 59.5 percent. [71]

Implications for Law Enforcement and Prosecutors

> **Performance Measure:** On the basis of victim reporting rates to law enforcement alone, law enforcement officers should be responding annually to at least 4 to 5 incidents per 1,000 females (12 and older) and 1 to 2 per 1,000 males (12 and older). On the basis of actual rates as determined by victim surveys, law enforcement officers should be responding annually to 8 to 9 incidents per 1,000 females, and 2 to 3 per 1,000 males. Therefore, if the incidence of domestic violence reported in victim surveys is significantly above the level that victims actually report to law enforcement, greater community outreach and barriers to reporting must be addressed. Law enforcement officers must encourage the rest of the community to do its part, and prosecutors must work with law enforcement if incidents are not making it into the courts. (Research basis: Confirmed by multiple national surveys over past decades, although exact rates [as opposed to the national average] may vary by region, population density, ethnicity of population, and so on.)

Implications for Judges

Judges typically see only a small minority of domestic violence cases that actually occur. (Research basis: Multiple studies across the country based on victim surveys, police arrest records and court cases.)

2.2 At what point do victims report domestic violence?

Victims do not generally report their initial intimate partner victimization but typically suffer multiple assaults or related victimizations before they contact authorities or apply for protective orders. [63, 105, 133] A Texas protective order study, like others conducted across the country, found that 68 percent of the victims taking out orders had been physically abused by their partners in the two years before they took out orders. [26] A Massachusetts arrest study found that a majority (55 percent) of sampled intimate partner victims who called police reported that either the frequency or the severity of ongoing abuse was increasing in the period before the call. Another 11 percent reported no increases in either frequency or severity but increased controlling behaviors such as restrictions on freedom of movement, access to money, medical or counseling services, or social support. [23] The NCVS found that victims were more likely to report reassaults than initial assaults. [63]

Implications for Law Enforcement

In questioning victims, law enforcement officers should always inquire about unreported *prior* assaults for evidence of crimes that may be charged, depending on the jurisdiction"s statute of limitations. These inquiries are also necessary to develop an accurate offender history to determine offender risk and to advise the victim. Prior abuse history may also be helpful in determining the primary or predominant aggressor. (Research basis: Both national studies and multiple, disparate individual-jurisdiction studies agree that battering that is likely to come to the attention of law enforcement constitutes repeated activity, much of it not reported to law enforcement initially.)

Implications for Prosecutors

In questioning victims, prosecutors should always inquire about prior unreported domestic violence for evidence of crimes that may be charged, depending on the jurisdiction"s statute of limitations, and/or are necessary to develop an accurate offender history to determine appropriate prosecution and sentencing recommendations. (Research basis: Both national studies and multiple, disparate individual-jurisdiction studies agree that battering that is likely to come to the attention of law enforcement constitutes repeated activity, much of it not reported to law enforcement initially.)

Implications for Judges

Judges should not assume that the civil petition or criminal case before them represents isolated, unique behaviors on the part of the involved parties, particularly the abuser. Although this assumption may not be relevant until after the specific petition or case has been decided, it must be considered in terms of fashioning remedies and sanctions. (Research basis: Both national and multiple, disparate individual-jurisdiction studies agree that battering that is likely to come to the attention of the criminal justice system represents repeated activity.)

2.3   Which victims are likely to report domestic violence?

Some victims are more likely to report their victimization or revictimization than others. Research indicates that women who have more experience with the criminal justice system — especially those with protective orders or who have experienced more severe abuse histories — are more likely to call police. [23, 27, 120, 141]

The seriousness of injury may not increase victim reporting, however, because of incapacity, the increased likelihood that a third party will call in these cases, or the fact that seriously injured victims are less likely to have protective orders. [23] Younger women, those in dating relationships, and those with little prior contact with the criminal justice system are less likely to call police. [23, 27]

Implications for Law Enforcement

When a victim reports domestic violence, it probably indicates repeated prior abuse incidents. Law enforcement officers should be trained in how to assist victims and encourage them to secure protective orders if for no other reason than victims with protective orders are more likely than those without such an order to alert police to subsequent victimization incidents. Existence of protective orders adds to the body of evidence for future prosecution. (Research basis: Both national surveys and multiple local studies conclude that victim reporting is not uniform or consistent. Although one might argue that protective orders generate violations by criminalizing otherwise legal behavior, both national and multiple local studies found higher reporting rates of a variety of domestic violence crimes for victims with protective orders.)

2.4   Does the quality of the law enforcement response influence whether domestic violence is reported?

Research indicates that actions of law enforcement, such as follow-up home visits after incidents, can encourage victim reports of domestic violence. [37] It appears that victim confidence in police response leads to more reports of new violence. [41, 68] This is reinforced by a study of a police department domestic violence unit, which documented that repeated victim contact with law enforcement officers assigned to a specialized domestic violence unit significantly increased the likelihood of victim reports of revictimization. [130]

On the other hand, research also shows that victims who reported prior victimization and thought the criminal justice response was insufficient or endangered them are less likely to report subsequent victimizations. [23] However, even if the victim opposed the arrest of her abuser, she is generally just as likely to report revictimizations as are victims who did not oppose the initial arrest. [23, 130]

Implications for Law Enforcement

Law enforcement officers should not be deterred from arresting abuse suspects for fear of prejudicing future victim reporting of revictimization. Law enforcement responses can increase victim reports of reabuse (even as they decrease the likelihood of reabuse). Therefore, increased reporting of victimization does not necessarily mean that law enforcement efforts are failing to reduce actual domestic abuse, and decreased reporting may not indicate successful law enforcement efforts. (Research basis: An increase in reported findings, based on three experimental studies as well as multiple observational studies from disparate localities.)

2.5 Who else reports domestic violence?

Most domestic violence reports are called in by victims, with victim report rates ranging from 59 percent [228] to 93 percent. [68] The review of NCVS reassaults between 1992 and 2002 found that 72 percent of the reassaults were reported by the victims, and 28 percent by third parties. [63] Third parties include family members, relatives and sometimes the suspects themselves. In Chicago"s domestic violence misdemeanor court, 26 percent of the calls were made by third parties on their own, and another 7.3 percent called at the direct behest of the victim. [107] Third parties are more likely to call police if the incident involved major injuries or a weapon. [23, 27] Other family members are significantly more likely to report abuse of elderly women (60 years and older) abused by other family members, usually sons, daughters or grandsons. [139]

Implications for Law Enforcement

Tapes of 911 domestic violence calls should be routinely maintained and accessible, as they may contain possible excited utterance evidence, because a majority of calls reporting incidents are made by victims (some of whom may be reluctant to testify later). In addition, the identities and contact information for third-party domestic violence callers should be elicited when possible in case they are potential witnesses. Dispatchers should be trained on these matters. (Research basis: Multiple national and local observational studies.)

Implications for Prosecutors

Prosecutors should ask law enforcement to catalog and maintain 911 tapes of domestic violence calls (since they may contain possible excited utterance evidence) because a majority of reported incidents are made by victims, some of whom may be reluctant to testify later. In addition, the identities and contact information for third-party domestic violence callers should be elicited when possible, in case they are potential incident witnesses. Dispatchers should be trained toward these ends, and this information should be forwarded to prosecutors. (Research basis: Multiple national and local observational studies.)

2.6 Are there other major sources for reports of domestic violence?

Unlike most crime victims, victims reporting domestic violence can use a parallel track, namely, civil courts where they can petition for protective/restraining orders. In many jurisdictions, more victims report intimate assaults and related crimes to civil courts than to law enforcement. [135] Research from both ends of the country, Massachusetts [32, 134] and the state of Washington

[121], however, indicates that the abuse reported in this civil setting is not significantly different from that reported to law enforcement.

Implications for Law Enforcement and Prosecutors

Civil protective order files offer law enforcement and prosecutors an essential tool in identifying domestic violence victims and perpetrators, gauging victim risk, and correctly calibrating appropriate charges and sentences. They may also indicate prior uncharged crimes that may be prosecuted along with more recent charges, particularly if the same victim and/or witnesses are involved in both sets of charges. They may also be used as evidence for violations of probationary sentences. Petitioner affidavits of abuse have been upheld as admissible evidence for probation violation in *Tweedie v. Garvey*, 94_CV_30139 (U.S. D. Springfield, MA, 1994). (Research basis: Disparate observational studies across the country as well as reported data from multiple states.)

Implications for Judges

Notwithstanding the court arena, civil or criminal, the abuse reported is typically as serious in one as in the other. The major differences are the responses courts can offer. For this reason, judges should inform or ensure that victims are informed that they may file criminal complaints in addition to petitioning courts for civil orders. Each process offers victims different benefits (and poses different challenges). (Research basis: Disparate observational studies across the country as well as reported data from multiple states.)

2.7 What kinds of domestic violence are reported to law enforcement and are prosecuted?

Notwithstanding varying numbers and types of crimes that constitute domestic violence in state codes and the U.S. Code, almost two-thirds to three-quarters of domestic violence cited in law enforcement incident reports are for assaults. [23, 68, 120, 196, 228] Although prosecutors screen cases, a study of domestic violence prosecutions in California, Oregon, Nebraska and Washington found that assaults constituted 59 to 81 percent of all prosecuted domestic violence cases. [196]

The percentage of felony assaults varies widely, reflecting specific state felony enhancement statutes. The highest percentage of felony assault domestic violence charges documented (41 percent) is in California, where injurious domestic assaults are classified as felonies. [228] However, most studies find much smaller percentages of felony assault charges — for instance, 13.7 percent in Charlotte, N.C. [68], and only 5.5 percent in Massachusetts [23] — as most physical injuries are minor and most cases do not involve the use of weapons.

These studies accord with the findings of the NCVS. [27] The NVCS, based on victim self-reports, not police characterizations, found simple assaults against female intimate partners to be more than four times greater (4.4) than aggravated assaults in 2005. Most assaults (80.5 percent) did not involve weapons. [27]

Implications for Law Enforcement

If the ratio of arrest reports for lesser offenses (such as disorderly conduct or breach of the peace) is significantly greater than that for assaults, it may indicate that patrol officers are not correctly identifying or assessing the underlying criminal behavior. Additional training or supervision may be required. (Research basis: Numerous observational studies from across the country as well as findings of national victim surveys, 1993-2004.)

Implications for Prosecutors

If the ratio of arrest reports for lesser offenses (such as disorderly conduct or breach of the peace) is significantly greater than that for assaults, it may indicate that local law enforcement is not correctly identifying the underlying criminal behavior. Prosecutors must work with officers to correctly determine the necessary elements of specific domestic violence crimes, including assault, stalking and marital rape. Alternatively, if the majority of domestic assaults are routinely pled down to lesser offenses by prosecutors, prosecutors may be endangering victims as well as failing to hold abusers fully accountable for their violence. Federal misdemeanor firearm prohibitions — 18 U.S.C. §922(g)(9), for example — only apply to assault convictions. Where enhancement statutes are available, prosecutors should carefully review prior convictions to charge defendants as repeat offenders where appropriate. (Research basis: Numerous observational studies from across the country as well as findings of national victim surveys, 1993-2004.)

Implications for Judges

Reducing assault charges to nonassault charges allows convicted abusers to retain firearms otherwise prohibited pursuant to federal law, 18 U.S.C. § 922(g)(9), which prohibits abusers convicted of misdemeanor assaults from possessing firearms or ammunition. Qualifying offenses must include the use or attempted use of physical force or the threatened use of a deadly weapon. Judges can facilitate application of the federal prohibition by making specific findings of these necessary elements required in the federal law. (Research basis: Numerous observational studies from across the country as well as findings of national victim surveys, 1993-2004.)

2.8 Do arrest rates correspond to actual rates of domestic violence and stalking based on victim surveys?

Domestic violence arrest rates as a percentage of written incident reports vary greatly because incident report writing practices vary across jurisdictions. A better, more consistent measure is the **arrests per capita** over the course of a year. At least one study documents that actual per capita arrests for domestic violence across an entire (albeit small) state exceeded the national estimates of domestic violence as determined by the NCVS. A Rhode Island study found in 2004 that per capita domestic violence arrests were 10.5 per 1,000 females (including both male and female suspects of female victims) and were 2.9 per 1,000 males (including both male and female suspects of male victims), higher than the national estimated incidence rates of 8.6 per 1,000 females and 2.5 per 1,000 males. [136] Other, disparate jurisdictions have similarly demonstrated high per capita arrest rates: Wichita, Kan. 12.1/1,000 (2000); Chicago, 6.9/1,000 (1997); and Nevada, 5.4/1,000 (2001). [135]

> **Performance Measure for Law Enforcement:** If domestic violence is broadly defined and if law enforcement agencies mandate and enforce arrest upon probable cause, over the course of a year, law enforcement can reach the same percentage of victims who identify themselves as abused in national crime victim surveys. Departments should establish benchmarks based on the NCVS to assess their performance. (Research basis: This performance measure is based on actual arrest figures from Rhode Island, a state with mandatory arrest for protective order violations and assaults with injuries, and where domestic violence includes any crime committed by family or household members, cohabitants, current or former intimate partners, and dating partners.

Jurisdictions" definitions will necessarily vary and are based on state laws as documented in Klein, 2004, pp. 90-91.)

2.9 Do stalking arrests correspond to actual stalking rates as reported by victims?

Stalking arrests are rare, nowhere near the estimated number of stalkers. [207] A pioneering study determined that, although 16.5 percent (in a sample of 1,731) of all domestic violence incident reports filed in Colorado Springs, Colo., involved stalking, in all but one incident the suspect was charged with a lesser offense — harassment, violation of a protective order, or another nonstalking domestic violence offense. [210]

Implications for Law Enforcement

If stalking arrests constitute a negligible proportion of all domestic violence arrests, departments should undertake a legal, policy and practice review to determine barriers to the enforcement of stalking statutes. Law enforcement officers should receive training on stalking behavior and statutes. Not only may charging abusers with stalking more accurately reflect their behavior but also stalking charges are more likely to constitute felonies in many jurisdictions than are alternative domestic offense charges. (Research basis: National surveys supplemented by multiple domestic violence arrest studies from disparate jurisdictions across the country.)

2.10 Is arrest the best response?

A major re-examination of a series of fairly rigorous experiments in multiple jurisdictions finds that arrest deters repeat reabuse, whether suspects are employed or not. In none of the sites was arrest associated with increased reabuse among intimate partners. [155] Another major study, based on 2,564 partner assaults reported in the NCVS (1992-2002), found that whether police arrested the suspect or not, their involvement had a strong deterrent effect. The positive effects of police involvement and arrest do not depend on whether the victim or a third party reported the incident to law enforcement. Neither do they depend on the seriousness of the incident assault, whether a misdemeanor or a felony. [63]

A Berkeley arrest study found similarly that all actions taken by responding officers — including arrest, providing victims with information pamphlets, taking down witness statements, and helping victims secure protective orders — were associated with reduced reabuse. By contrast, the highest reabuse rates were found where the responding officers left it to the victim to make a "citizen arrest," swearing out a complaint herself. [228] Research has also shown that police response also significantly increases the likelihood that victims will secure protective orders. [130, 151, 152]

Research also finds that, by and large, the vast majority of victims report satisfaction with the arrest of their abuser when interviewed after the fact. In Massachusetts, 82 percent were either very or somewhat satisfied, and 85.4 percent said they would call police again for a similar incident. [23] Similarly, a study of courts in California, Oregon, Nebraska and Washington found that 76 percent of the victims said they wanted their abuser arrested. [196] Also important to note is that police arrests in spite of victims" objections do not reduce the likelihood of victims reporting new abuse to police. [5]

Implications for Law Enforcement

Arrest should be the default position for law enforcement in all domestic violence incidents. (Research basis: Multiple studies in diverse jurisdictions. The police arrest studies were combined carefully, and intimate partner abuse cases were separated from family abuse cases.)

Implications for Prosecutors and Judges

One of the best ways prosecutors can encourage law enforcement to arrest abuser suspects is to follow through where possible by filing charges against those arrested. Judges encourage the arrest of abusers by ensuring that domestic violence cases that reach court are heard and not dismissed out of hand. (Research basis: The efficacy of arrests has been widely researched; the influence of prosecutors on law enforcement arrest behavior has been found in studies in which pro-arrest departmental policies mitigated anti-arrest personal views of individual officers. [59])

2.11 What should law enforcement's response be if the suspect is gone when they arrive?

A large percentage of alleged abusers leave the crime scene before law enforcement arrives. Where noted, absence rates range from 42 to 66 percent. [23, 50, 117, 196, 227, 228] Pursuing alleged abusers, including the issuance of warrants, is associated with reduced revictimization. [50] Pursuing absent suspects may be of particular utility because limited research finds that suspects who flee the scene before police arrive are significantly more likely to have prior criminal histories and to reabuse than those arrested at the scene. [23] Similarly, another study finds higher reabuse *if the victim is gone* when officers arrive. [228]

Implications for Law Enforcement

Law enforcement officers should make the arrest of abusers who flee the scene a priority. (Research basis: Numerous studies confirm that a large proportion of abusers flee the scene; only one study has looked at differences in records of those who fled the scene and those who didn't.)

> **Performance Measure:** According to a national survey, 68 percent of police departments have specific policies that cover policies and procedures for responding law enforcement officers if the perpetrator is gone when they arrive. [213] In a study of the south shore communities of Massachusetts, researchers documented that police arrested 100 percent of abusers present at the scene and arrested or issued warrants for a majority (54 percent) who left the scene, for a total arrest or warrant rate of about 75 percent. [23] Similarly, a statewide New York study found that half of the domestic violence suspects fled the scene, but local police ultimately arrested 60 percent of those who fled. [165] (Research basis: State law varies regarding the power of police to arrest after the incident. Time limits are not restricted in Massachusetts or New York, where these results were documented.)

Implications for Prosecutors

Prosecutors should encourage law enforcement officers to file warrants for abusers who flee the scene and prepare reports for subsequent prosecution when arrests are made. Similarly, prosecutors should assist victims to file criminal complaints if necessary to allow for the prosecution of abusers who have left the scene before police arrived. (Research basis:

Numerous studies confirm that a large proportion of abusers flee the scene. Only one study has looked at differences in records of those who fled the scene and those who didn't.)

2.12 Who is the primary/predominant aggressor?

A substantial percentage of victims of domestic violence hit their perpetrators back. [72] In Massachusetts, 37.3 percent of the female victims fought back in the incident in which their male abuser was arrested. However, most (59.1 percent) of those females who fought back found that this made their abuser more violent. [23] A substantial number of victims will not self-disclose their victimization. [93] Consequently, determination of primary or predominant aggressor may not be self-evident. Nonetheless, data on police action in 2,819 jurisdictions in 19 states reveal that only 1.9 percent of incidents resulted in dual arrests for intimate partner violence and intimidation. In other words, less than 4 percent of all intimate partner arrests were dual arrests in which law enforcement could not determine a primary or predominant aggressor. [117]

Studies suggest that officers" determination of primary or predominant aggressor is particularly problematic when the intimate partner violence occurs between same-sex couples. Although police are equally likely to make arrests in same-sex as in heterosexual partner abuse cases, a study of more than 1,000 same-sex intimate partner violence reports from departments across the country found that officers were substantially more likely to arrest both parties in same-sex cases. Specifically, 26.1 percent of female same-sex cases and 27.3 percent of male same-sex cases resulted in dual arrests, compared to only 0.8 percent with male offenders and female victims, and 3 percent with female offenders and male victims. [175]

Research on the impact of primary aggressor policies, either mandated by state statute or by individual law enforcement agencies, reveals that such policies significantly reduce the percentage of dual arrests from an average of 9 percent to 2 percent of domestic violence arrests. [117]

Implications for Law Enforcement

If the rate of dual arrests exceeds that found on average across the country, law enforcement departments should develop and implement specific primary aggressor policies and protocols. (Research basis: The most significant dual-arrest study was based on examination of all assault and intimidation cases in the 2000 National Incident-Based Reporting System (NIBRS) database as well as more detailed examination of these data from 25 diverse police departments across the country.)

Implications for Prosecutors

If presented with a dual-arrest case, prosecutors should conduct an independent analysis to determine the predominant aggressor and proceed against that suspect alone. Determination of primary/predominant aggressor is briefly described by the American Prosecutors Research Institute on its Web site: http://www.ndaa.org/apri/programs/vawa/dv_101.html. (Research basis: The most significant dual-arrest study documenting its rarity was based on examination of all assault and intimidation cases in the 2000 NIBRS database as well as more detailed examination of these data from 25 diverse police departments across the country.)

Implications for Judges

In dual-arrest cases, judges should insist that prosecutors provide evidence that one of the parties was the primary or predominant aggressor and the other the victim. This may be particularly important, as advocates caution that female victims who are arrested along with their abusers may nonetheless plead guilty in order to be able to return home to care for minor children. Furthermore, it appears that law enforcement finds it particularly challenging to determine the primary/predominant aggressor with same-sex couples. (Research basis: The most significant dual-arrest study was based on examination of all assault and intimidation cases in the 2000 NIBRS database as well as more detailed examination of these data from 25 diverse police departments across the country.)

3. Perpetrator Characteristics

3.1 What is their gender?

Although some sociological research [202] based on self-reporting finds equal rates of male and female partner **conflict** (including mostly minor physical assaults), behavior that is likely to violate most state and federal criminal and civil (protective order) statutes is typically perpetrated by males. [153]

Perpetrators that come to the attention of the criminal justice system are overwhelmingly male. For example, 86 percent of abusers brought to court for restraining orders in Massachusetts were male, [2] as were those arrested for domestic violence in California [228] and Charlotte, N.C. (as much as 97.4 percent for the most serious cases). [68] In Rhode Island, 92 percent of abusers placed on probation for domestic violence were male. [68, 141] A Cincinnati court study found 86.5 percent of 2,670 misdemeanor domestic violence court defendants to be male. [11] The overwhelming majority of their victims were women: 84 percent in both Charlotte, N.C., [68] and Berkeley, Calif. [228] The 2000 NIBRS multistate study found that 81 percent of the suspects were male and their victims were female. [117]

Jurisdictions with higher numbers of female suspects and male victims usually include higher numbers of non-intimate family violence cases. [139, 196] The latter typically involve older victims and their adult children perpetrators. A study of elder abuse across the state of Rhode Island, for example, found that two-thirds of elder female victims were abused by family members as opposed to intimate partners, including 46.2 percent by adult sons and 26.9 percent by adult daughters, 8.6 percent by grandsons and 1.6 percent by granddaughters. [139]

Implications for Law Enforcement

If the ratio of male to female suspects and victims differs substantially from those found above, departments should be alert to potential gender bias in their response to domestic violence. Ongoing training and supervision can address overrepresentation of female versus male arrests. (Research basis: Multiple studies of abusers and their victims brought to the attention of the criminal justice system [including civil protective orders] confirm the gender ratio as opposed to studies focusing on non-intimate and family conflict.)

Implications for Prosecutors

Prosecutors should be alert to gender bias in the response of local law enforcement agencies and re-screen cases if the percentage of female suspects accused of abusing male victims exceeds that commonly found across the nation. (Research basis: Multiple studies of abusers and their victims brought to the attention of the criminal justice system [including civil protective orders] confirm the gender ratio as opposed to studies focusing on non-intimate and family conflict.)

Implications for Judges

If, upon reviewing domestic violence dockets, judges find much higher rates of female-on-male abuse cases than those typically found across the country as a whole, they should be alert to potential gender bias on the part of police and/or prosecutors and ensure that they are presented with sufficient evidence to confirm the correct designation of victims and their abusers. (Research basis: Multiple studies of abusers and their victims brought to the attention of the criminal justice system [including civil protective orders] confirm the gender ratio as opposed to studies focusing on non-intimate and family conflict.)

3.2 What age are they?

Most studies find most perpetrators to be between 18 and 35 years old, with a median age of about 33 years, although they range in age from 13 to 81. [11, 23, 68, 228] A large U.S. west coast study of abusers subject to police incident reports or protective orders found that 33 percent were between 20 and 29 years old, and slightly more (33.4 percent) were between 30 and 39 years old. [121]

3.3 Are they likely to be known to law enforcement already?

Most studies agree that the majority of domestic violence perpetrators that come to the attention of criminal justice or court authorities have a prior criminal history for a variety of nonviolent and violent offenses against males as well as females, and of a domestic or nondomestic nature. For example, a study of intimate partner arrests in Connecticut, Idaho and Virginia of more than 1,000 cases each found that almost 70 percent (69.2) had a prior record and that 41.8 percent of those had been convicted of a violent crime, including robbery and rape. [117]

The percentage of officially identified perpetrators with criminal histories ranges from a low of 49 percent for prior arrest within five years in an arrest study in Portland, Ore. [130], to 89 percent for at least one prior nonviolent misdemeanor arrest for domestic violence defendants arraigned in a Toledo, Ohio, Municipal Court. [216] Not only did most of the abusers brought to the Toledo Court for domestic violence have a prior arrest history but the average number of prior arrests was 14. Similarly, 84.4 percent of men arrested for domestic violence in Massachusetts had prior criminal records, averaging a little more than 13 prior charges (resulting from five to six arrests) — including four for property offenses, three for offenses against persons, three for major motor vehicle offenses, two for alcohol/drug offenses, one for public order violations, and 0.14 for sex offenses. [23] A study of the Cook County (Chicago) misdemeanor domestic violence court found that 57 percent of the men charged with misdemeanor domestic violence had prior records for drug offenses, 52.3 percent for theft, 68.2 percent for public order offenses, and 61.2 percent for property crimes. On average, they had 13 prior arrests. [107]

Even if abusers have no prior arrest records, they may be known to local police. In North Carolina, for example, researchers found from police files that 67.7 percent of the domestic violence arrestees had prior contact with the local criminal justice system, 64.5 percent were officially known by local police, and 48.3 percent had prior domestic violence incident reports. [68]

Studies of abusers brought to court for protective orders find similarly high rates of criminal histories, ranging from slightly more than 70 percent in Texas [26] to 80 percent in Massachusetts. [134]

Implications for Law Enforcement, Prosecutors and Judges

Given the large overlap between domestic violence and general criminality, law enforcement should carefully check domestic violence suspects" status in regard to outstanding warrants, pending cases, probationary or parole status, and other concurrent criminal justice involvement, including suspect involvement as a confidential informant for ongoing investigations. With regard to the latter, in the event the informant is involved in a domestic violence incident, he should be precluded from working with the department without the authorization of department supervisors. In prosecuting or sentencing defendants for other crimes, prosecutors and judges should look for concurrent domestic violence that was previously prosecuted, is pending, or that may be charged. (Research basis: Multiple studies from jurisdictions across the country confirm these findings, although the extent of prior records may vary, depending on jurisdictional law enforcement, court practices and resources.)

3.4 Are they likely to be drug and/or alcohol abusers?

As with criminality in general, there is a high correlation between alcohol and substance abuse and domestic violence for abusers. This is not to say that substance abuse causes domestic violence. The Memphis night arrest study found that 92 percent of assailants used drugs or alcohol on the day of the assault, and nearly half were described by families as daily substance abusers for the prior month. [19] Other studies found a lower but still substantial incidence of substance use. For example, a California arrest study found alcohol or drugs, or both, were involved in 38 percent of the domestic violence incident arrests. [228] A large Seattle arrest and protective order study found that alcohol/drug use was reported in 24.1 percent of incidents involving police. [120, 121] It was higher in North Carolina, where 45 percent of suspects were identified as being intoxicated. [68]

A domestic violence fatality review study in New Mexico documented that alcohol and drugs were present in 65 percent of 46 domestic violence homicides between 1993 and 1996: 43 percent abused alcohol and 22 percent abused drugs. [170] Two surveys, one of state correctional facilities in 1991 and the other of jails in 1995, found more than half of those jailed or imprisoned for domestic violence admitted drinking and/or using drugs at the time of the incident. [93] Self-reports from batterers in Chicago revealed that 15 to 19 percent admitted to having a drug problem, and 26 to 31 percent scored more than one on the CAGE (Cut down drinking, drinking Annoyed others, felt Guilt over drinking, and needed a morning Eye-opener drink) test indicating alcohol abuse. [12] Among defendants prosecuted in Chicago"s domestic violence misdemeanor court, 60.7 percent were found to have "ever had an alcohol or drug problem." [107]

Interviews with more than 400 North Carolina female victims who called police for misdemeanor domestic assaults found that abuser drunkenness was the most consistent predictor of a call to police. According to the victims, almost a quarter (23 percent) of the abusers "very often" or "almost always" got drunk when they drank, more than half (55 percent) were binge drinkers, 29.3 percent used cocaine at least once a month, and more than a third (39 percent) smoked marijuana. Furthermore, almost two-thirds of abusers were drinking at the scene of the incident, having consumed an average of almost seven drinks, resulting in more than half of them (58 percent) being drunk. [126] The national crime victims survey found substantial, but lesser rates of substance abuse. Between 1993 and 2004, victims reported that 43 percent of all nonfatal intimate partner violence involved the presence of alcohol or drugs, another 7 percent involved both alcohol and drugs, and 6 percent involved drugs alone. [27]

Both a batterer and an alcohol treatment study similarly reveal a consistent, high correlation between alcohol abuse and domestic violence. In one study, for example, for 272 males entering treatment for battering or alcoholism, the odds of any male-to-female aggression were 8 to 11 times higher on days they drank than on days they did not. [56]

Implications for Law Enforcement

Law enforcement officers should note the use of alcohol or drugs in domestic violence incident reports, not to mitigate abusive behavior but to indicate heightened abuser risk for continued abuse. (Research basis: The correlation is found in multiple studies across the country.)

Implications for Prosecutors and Judges

The presence of drug and/or alcohol abuse makes continued offending more likely. Although sobriety may not eliminate the risk for reabuse, research suggests it may be a necessary ingredient. When recommending or setting release or sentence conditions, requiring abstinence from alcohol and drugs may be appropriate. (Research basis: Correlation is found in multiple studies across the country.)

3.5 Are they likely to be mentally ill or have certain personality traits?

Batterers are no more likely to be mentally ill than the general population. [89] Although various researchers have attempted to classify abusers — ranging from agitated "pit bulls" and silent "cobras" [128] to "dysphoric/borderline" and "generally violent and anti-social" [122] — attempts to use these classifications to predict risk of reabuse have proven unhelpful. [112] However, researchers agree that batterers may differ markedly from each other. [29, 123, 193] Although some batterers may appear to be emotionally overwrought to responding police officers, other batterers may appear calm and collected. [128] Other research suggests that batterers can be classified as low-, moderate- and high-level abusers and that, contrary to common belief, batterers remain within these categories. [28] Similarly, in the treatment literature, the multistate study of four batterer intervention programs consistently found that approximately a quarter of court-referred batterers are high-level abusers, unlikely to respond to treatment. [84, 85, 88]

Implications for Law Enforcement

Abuser demeanor at the scene, especially compared to overwrought, traumatized victims, can be misleading. (Research basis: Multiple studies have failed to validate any classification of battering propensity based on personality types or mental illnesses, and multiple observational studies reveal different patterns of behaviors among batterers.)

Implications for Prosecutors and Judges

Battering does not appear to be a mental aberration and is not responsive to mental health counseling. Although batterers may suffer from depression or low self-esteem after being arrested or restrained, these conditions have not been found to have caused the abuse. (Research basis: Multiple studies have failed to validate any classification of battering propensity based on personality types or mental illnesses, and multiple observational studies reveal different patterns of behaviors among batterers.)

3.6 Do abusers stick with one victim?

Deprived of their victim, many abusers will go on to abuse another intimate partner or family member. Others may abuse multiple intimate partners and family members simultaneously. [32] The Rhode Island probation study, for example, found that in a one-year period, more than a quarter (28 percent) of those probationers who were rearrested for a new crime of domestic violence abused a different partner or family member. [141] The Massachusetts study of persons arrested for violating a civil restraining order found that almost half (43 percent) had **two or more victims over six years**. [18] This confirms an earlier state study finding that 25 percent of individuals who had protective orders taken out against them in 1992 had up to eight new orders taken out against them by as many victims over the subsequent six years. [2]

Studies have generally found that abusers who go on to abuse new partners are not substantially different from those who reabuse the same partner, with the exception that they tend to be younger and are not married to their partners. [2, 141]

Implications for Law Enforcement, Prosecutors and Judges

If the abuser is no longer with the victim of the last domestic violence incident, new intimate partners are vulnerable to becoming new targets of abuse. Whether the batterer remains with the same victim or not, battering behavior brought to police and prosecutors" attention is likely to reflect chronic, patterned, non-isolated behavior that is victim specific. In charging decisions, sentencing recommendations, and fashioning protective orders or criminal sanctions, prosecutors and judges must be concerned with future intimate-partner victims as well as immediate victims, even if the immediate intimate-partner victims are no longer available to the abusers. (Research basis: Although longitudinal studies of batterers are few, multiple studies that follow batterers for only a year or two also confirm the serial nature of battering for some abusers.)

3.7 How many abusers are likely to do it again?

Depending on how reabuse is measured, over what period of time, and what countermeasures either the victim (e.g., getting a protective order or going into hiding) or the criminal justice system takes (arresting or locking up the abuser), a hard core of approximately one-third of abusers will reabuse in the short run, and more will reabuse in the long run.

In Rhode Island, 38.4 percent of abusers were arrested for a new domestic violence offense within two years of being placed on probation supervision for a misdemeanor domestic violence offense. [141] A half-dozen batterer program studies published between 1988 and 2001 and conducted across the United States documented reabuse, as reported by victims, ranging from 26 to 41 percent within five to 30 months. [4, 48, 54, 84, 85, 88, 89, 98] Five studies published between 1985 and 1999 of court-restrained abusers in multiple states found reabuse rates, as measured by arrest and victim reports for the period of four months to two years after their last abuse offense, to range from 24 to 60 percent. [4, 26, 105, 133, 134]

Where studies have found substantially lower rearrest rates for abuse, it appears the lower rate is a result of police behavior, not abuser behavior. In these jurisdictions, victims report equivalent reabuse, notwithstanding low rearrest rates. For example, studies of more than 1,000 female victims in Florida, New York City and Los Angeles found that, whereas only 4 to 6 percent of their abusers were arrested for reabuse within one year, 31 percent of the victims reported being physically abused during the following year (one-half of those reporting being burned, strangled, beaten up or seriously injured) and 16 percent reported being stalked or threatened. [61, 190] Similarly, in a Bronx domestic court study, whereas only 14 to 15 percent of defendants convicted of domestic violence misdemeanors or violations were rearrested after one year, victims reported reabuse rates of 48 percent during that year. [185]

Reabuse has found to be substantially higher in longer term studies. A Massachusetts study tracked 350 male abusers arrested for abusing their female intimate partners over a decade, 1995 to 2005. The study found that 60 percent were rearrested for a new domestic assault or had a protective order taken out against them, even though some went three to four years between arrests. [138, 224] An equivalently high rearrest rate for domestic violence was also documented in Colorado between 1994 and 2005. During that time, of 84,431 defendants arrested for domestic violence, according to the state bureau of investigation, more than 50,000 (nearly 60 percent) were arrested for domestic violence charges more than once. In other words, the domestic violence rearrest rate was almost 60 percent for arrested abusers over an average of five years. [125]

Implications for Law Enforcement

It is safe to assume that, more often than not, the typical abuser who comes to the attention of law enforcement has a high likelihood of continuing to abuse the same or a different victim, both in the short term and over the subsequent decade at least. (Research basis: Although observational studies vary on reports of reabuse [depending on how it is measured], there is widespread consensus that reported reabuse is substantially less than actual reabuse experienced by victims, which is typically found to be more than 50 percent. The few longitudinal studies of more than a year or two suggest that many abusers continue to abuse, notwithstanding gaps of several years between initial and subsequent reported incidents.)

Implications for Prosecutors and Judges

It is safe to assume that, more often than not, the typical abuser who makes it to the prosecutor"s office has a high likelihood of continuing to abuse the same or a different victim, both in the short term and over the subsequent decade at least. While prosecuting specific, discrete incidents, prosecutors should recommend sentences that address long-term patterns of criminal behavior and are based on abuser risk for reabuse. Judges should fashion civil or criminal remedies/sanctions that maximize protection of current and/or future victims from the abuser. It is inappropriate to consider a repeat abuser as a "first" offender just because several years may have passed between abuse offenses. (Research basis: Although observational studies vary on reports of reabuse [depending on how it is measured], there is widespread consensus that reported reabuse is substantially less than actual reabuse experienced by victims, which is typically found to be more than 50 percent. The few longitudinal studies of more than a year or two suggest that many abusers continue to abuse, notwithstanding gaps of several years between initial and subsequent reported incidents.)

3.8 Are abusers at risk for committing new nondomestic violence crimes?

Given their extensive prior criminal histories, abusers typically do not confine their reoffending to domestic violence alone. Studies concur that abusers are also likely to commit new nondomestic violence crimes in addition to domestic-violence-related crimes. Two New York City studies, one in the Bronx Misdemeanor Domestic Violence Court and the other in the Brooklyn Felony Domestic Violence Court, found that 58 percent of those arrested for domestic violence were rearrested for any crime within 30 months of the study arrest in the former study [164], and 44 percent within two years of arrest in the latter. [183] Most of the new arrests (according to official complaints) were for nondomestic-violence-related crimes such as drug possession/sale or property offenses.

Similarly, whereas 51 percent of Massachusetts abuser arrestees were rearrested for new domestic violence over the following 10 years, 57 percent were rearrested for nondomestic violence, including 15 percent who were not also arrested for new domestic violence. [138] Among Cook County domestic violence misdemeanants, 26.1 percent were arrested within 2.4 years on average for new domestic violence, whereas 46.5 percent were arrested for any offense. [12]

It is not surprising that research from the National Youth Survey found that most men (76 percent) who engage in domestic violence report also engaging in one or more deviant acts concurrently, including illegal behavior such as stealing or illicit drug use. [167] Nor is it surprising that abuser violence was not limited to their households. In Cook County (Chicago), the majority of prosecuted misdemeanor domestic violence offenders (55.6 percent) were found to have been violent with others as well as their partners. [107]

Implications for Law Enforcement, Prosecutors and Judges

Aggressively pursuing, prosecuting and sentencing abusers not only may protect victims and their children but also may reduce nondomestic offenses often committed by abusers. (Research basis: Although multiple, disparate studies document that abusers identified by the criminal justice system are likely to have nondomestic criminal histories, at least one study of nonarrested young married or cohabiting men also found that domestic violence and other deviant behaviors were associated both concurrently and prospectively.)

3.9 When are abusers likely to reabuse?

Studies agree that for those abusers who reoffend, a majority do so relatively quickly. In states where no-contact orders are automatically imposed after an arrest for domestic violence, rearrests for order violations begin to occur immediately upon the defendant"s release from the police station or court. For example, in both a Massachusetts misdemeanor arrest study and a Brooklyn, N.Y., felony arrest study, the majority of defendants rearrested for new abuse were arrested while their initial abuse cases were still pending in court. [23, 164] The latter included a 16-percent arrest rate for violation of no-contact orders and a 14-percent arrest rate for a new felony offense. [164] Similarly, a little more than one-third of the domestic violence probationers in Rhode Island who were rearrested for domestic violence were rearrested within two months of being placed under probation supervision. More than half (60 percent) were arrested within six months. [141] A multistate study of abusers referred to batterer programs found that almost half of the men (44 percent) who reassaulted their partners did so within three months of batterer program intake, and two-thirds within six months. The men who reassaulted within the first three months were more likely to repeatedly reassault their partners than the men who committed the first reassault after the first three months. [81, 83, 84] In the Bronx, similarly, reoffending happened early among those convicted for misdemeanor or domestic violence violations. Of those rearrested for domestic violence, approximately two-thirds reoffended within the first six months. [185]

Implications for Law Enforcement

Arrest is only the first step in stopping abuse. Countermeasures must begin immediately, once the suspect is released pending trial. Focusing on those already arrested for domestic violence provides law enforcement with the means to target a high-risk population of abusers who are disproportionately likely to commit new abuse-related and other offenses. (Research basis: Multiple studies from disparate jurisdictions have all found relatively quick reabuse by abusers who reabuse within the first year or two.)

Implications for Prosecutors and Judges

Arrest is only the first step in stopping abuse. Once arrested, prosecutors must immediately pursue measures to safeguard victims pending trial and thereafter. If abusers are automatically released pending trial, the most vulnerable victims will be reabused by the worst abusers. This reabuse may also inhibit subsequent victim cooperation with prosecutors, resulting in subsequent dismissals for lack of prosecution. This in turn may further encourage abusers to continue their abuse. (Research basis: Multiple studies from disparate jurisdictions have all found relatively quick reabuse by those that reabuse within the first year or two.)

3.10 Which abusers are likely to do it again in the short term?

When officers respond to a domestic violence call, they typically do not have a lot of information about the parties involved, their psychological profiles, family and child development histories, and the like. Fortunately, the research consistently finds that the basic information usually available to officers provides as accurate a prediction of abuser risk to the victim as do more extensive and time-consuming investigations involving more sources (e.g., clinical assessments). [111, 112, 113, 189] As a Bronx study on batterer treatment concluded, intensive individual assessments of attitudes or personality are not required to make reasonable judgments regarding abusers" risk of reabuse. [183]

3.11 Is gender an important risk factor?

Of course, the most powerful predictor of risk of domestic violence is gender. All of the research concurs that males are more likely to reabuse than females. [183]

3.12 Is age an important risk factor?

Younger defendants are more likely to reabuse and recidivate than older defendants. [23, 141, 183, 185, 216, 228] This has been found to be true in studies of arrested abusers and batterers in treatment programs as well as court-restrained abusers. [111, 112, 134, 153, 228]

3.13 Is prior arrest history an important risk factor?

If the abuser has just *one* prior arrest on his criminal record for *any* crime (not just domestic violence), he is more likely to reabuse than if he has no prior arrest. [23, 39, 85, 172, 185] A multistate study of more than 3,000 police arrests found that offenders with a prior arrest record for any offense were more than *seven* times more likely to be rearrested than those without prior records. [117]

The length of prior record is predictive of reabuse as well as general recidivism. [163] In looking at all restrained male abusers over two years, Massachusetts research documented that if the restrained abuser had just one prior arrest for any offense on his criminal record, his reabuse rate of the same victim rose from 15 to 25 percent; if he had five to six prior arrests, it rose to 50 percent. [134] In the Rhode Island abuser probation study, abusers with one prior arrest for any crime were almost twice as likely to reabuse within one year, compared to those with no prior arrest (40 percent vs. 22.6 percent). If abusers had more than one prior arrest, reabuse increased to 73.3 percent. [141] Of course, prior civil or criminal records specifically for abuse also increase the likelihood for reabuse. [23, 68, 216, 228]

Related to the correlation between prior arrest history and reabuse, research also finds similar increased risk for reabuse if suspects are on warrants. In the Berkeley study, researchers documented that having a pending warrant at the time of a domestic violence incident for a prior nondomestic violence offense was a better predictor of reabuse than a prior domestic violence record alone. [228] Similarly, in the one study that addressed this issue, suspects who were gone when police arrived were twice as likely to reabuse as those found on the scene by police. [23]

Similarly, one large statewide study found that if the suspect before the court for domestic violence was already on probation for anything else, or if another domestic violence case was also pending at the time of a subsequent arrest for domestic violence, that defendant was more likely to be arrested again for domestic violence within one year. [141]

Implications for Law Enforcement

The absence of a prior domestic violence arrest is not as powerful a predictor of no reabuse as the absence of a prior arrest for anything. On the other hand, a prior arrest record for any crime may be as accurate a predictor for subsequent domestic violence as a prior record for domestic violence. Law enforcement officers should attempt to track down the suspect who leaves the scene and aggressively serve warrants to protect victims from higher risk abusers. (Research basis: Multiple studies in disparate jurisdictions find that both prior criminal history and prior domestic violence correlate with reabuse, and vice versa, although the predictive power of prior domestic violence history may be less revealing if domestic violence arrest rates are low in that specific jurisdiction. Although only the limited studies speak to reabuse in correlation with abuser flight, they are consistent with more plentiful arrest studies that find support for the efficacy of arresting abuse suspects.)

Implications for Prosecutors and Judges

The absence of a prior domestic violence arrest is not as powerful a predictor of no reabuse as the absence of a prior arrest for anything. On the other hand, a prior arrest record for any crime is as accurate a predictor of subsequent domestic violence as a prior record for domestic violence. Therefore, in making charging decisions and sentencing recommendations, prosecutors should understand that if an abuser has a prior record for any crime, the prosecutor should assume him to be a high-risk domestic violence offender, not a low-risk "first" offender. Prosecutors should carefully review defendants" prior arrest records for warrant status and bail status at the time of the domestic violence arrest to accurately gauge defendant risk. Judges should understand that if an abuser has a prior record for *any* crime, he is a high-risk domestic-violence offender, not a low-risk "first" offender. Judges should demand access to prior criminal and abuse histories before fashioning civil orders, making pretrial release decisions, or sentencing abusers. (Research basis: Multiple studies in disparate jurisdictions find both prior criminal history and prior domestic violence correlate with reabuse, and vice versa, although the predictive power of prior domestic violence history may be less revealing if domestic violence arrest rates are low in that specific jurisdiction.)

3.14 Is substance abuse an important risk factor?

Acute and chronic alcohol and drug use are well-established risk factors for reabuse as well as domestic violence in general. [118, 221] Prior arrests for drug and alcohol offenses also correlate with higher rates of reabuse. [78] Just one prior arrest for any alcohol or drug offense (e.g., drunk driving or possession of a controlled substance), for example, doubled the reabuse rate from 20 percent (no prior drug/alcohol arrest) to 40 percent (at least one arrest for drugs/alcohol) in a restraining order study over two years. [134]

Defendant alcohol and substance abuse, similarly, are predictive of reabuse and recidivism. [23, 134, 141, 228] The multistate batterer program referral study found heavy drinking to be a significant predictor for reabuse. For the same reason, it found that abuser participation in drug treatment predicted repeated reassaults. [113] Batterers who complete batterer intervention are three times more likely to reabuse if they are found to be intoxicated when tested at three-month intervals. [83, 84, 85, 88]

Many [63, 117, 172], but not all, studies [23] have found abuser or victim abuse of drugs or alcohol *at the time of the incident* to be a consistent risk marker for continued abuse.

Implications for Law Enforcement

Seemingly unrelated nonviolent offenses such as drunk driving or drug possession, which suggest substance abuse by the abuser, should be considered as risk markers for continued abuse. (Research basis: Multiple, disparate studies suggest that any disagreement regarding the relationship between domestic abuse and substance abuse has to do with whether or not substance abuse "causes" domestic violence, not with the existence of the correlation.)

Implications for Prosecutors and Judges

Seemingly unrelated nonviolent offenses like drunk driving or drug possession, which suggest substance abuse by the abuser, should be considered as risk markers for continued abuse. Substance and alcohol abuse should be considered when prosecutors make prerelease and sentencing recommendations and when judges set bail, pronounce sentences, and fashion civil protective orders and conditions of probation supervision. (Research basis: Multiple, disparate studies suggest that any disagreement regarding the relationship between domestic abuse and substance abuse has to do with whether or not substance abuse "causes" domestic violence, not with the existence of the correlation.)

3.15 Are victims accurate predictors of reabuse?

Victim perception of risk has been found to significantly improve the accuracy of prediction over other risk factors [44], increasing *sensitivity* — the proportion of true positives that are correctly identified by the test — from 55 to 70 percent. [112] However, the same researchers found that women"s perceptions have to be interpreted. Women who felt very safe were less likely to be repeatedly reassaulted than those that felt somewhat safe. However, women who were uncertain or felt somewhat unsafe were more likely to be reassaulted repeatedly than those who felt they were in great danger. The reason for this apparent contradiction is that women who felt in greatest danger took effective countermeasures during the study. In other words, the research suggests that if women are not certain they will be safe, they err by giving the benefit of the doubt to their abuser. For these reasons, these researchers concluded that the best predictions of repeated reassaults were obtained by using risk markers, including women"s perceptions. [44, 112] The researchers" concern for victims with regard to assessed risk of abuse is borne out by a study of more than 1,000 women who sought protective orders or shelter, or whose abusers were arrested in Los Angeles or New York City. Almost a quarter of the victims who thought their risk of reassault was low were, in fact, reassaulted within one year. [190]

Victims" perception of risk also affects their reaction to criminal justice intervention. Arrest research finds that victims who were not revictimized for more than two years were twice as likely to have opposed arrest, compared to those who were revictimized. Those victims who thought police and court intervention did not go far enough were also accurate. Those who said police actions were too weak were three times more likely to experience revictimization, and those victims who said courts failed them were seven times more likely to experience revictimization. [23]

Implications for Law Enforcement

Asking victims if they fear reassault or severe reassaults provides one of the best ways to predict reabuse or potential lethality — and requires the least resources and time commitment

— but cannot be relied on exclusively as a predictor. Although women are unlikely to exaggerate their risk, they often underestimate it. (Research basis: A national homicide study involving hundreds of victims of attempted homicides, as well as the general reabuse studies, confirms these findings.)

Implications for Prosecutors and Judges

Victim input should be an important part of any risk calculation considered by prosecutors and judges. If victims are in doubt as to their safety, prosecutors and judges should assume the worst. (Research basis: Extensive examination of multiple domestic violence risk studies shows agreement on this point.)

3.16 Are there other common risk factors associated with reabuse?

Several studies have found other consistent risk markers for reabuse, many associated with the variables described above. These include increased risk associated with abusers who flee the scene of domestic violence [23]; abusers who are unemployed [13, 25, 142, 154, 172], economically disadvantaged and living in disadvantaged neighborhoods [153], or living in a household with firearms [25, 142]; or abusers who are not the fathers of children in the household. [25, 142]

Implications for Law Enforcement

Law enforcement officers recording the status of the above variables in their initial reports will provide valuable data for the determination of risk in future bail hearings, charging decisions and sentencing reports. (Research basis: These specific risk factors generally have been found in multiple studies but may vary in relevance and power across jurisdictions.)

Implications for Prosecutors and Judges

Prosecutors and judges should review the status of the above variables for determination of risk to be used in bail hearings, charging decisions, sentencing recommendations and decisions, and fashioning civil protective orders and conditions of probation supervision. (Research basis: These specific risk factors generally have been found in multiple studies but may vary in relevance and power across jurisdictions.)

3.17 What factors are not associated with reabuse?

Generally, the seriousness of the presenting incident does not predict reabuse, whether felony or misdemeanor, including whether there were injuries or not, or what the specific charge is. [23, 39, 134, 141, 145, 172] Abuser personality types have not been found to be associated with increased risk of reabuse. [113] Actuarial data offer improvement over clinical data. [189] Victim characteristics, including relationship with abuser, marital status, and whether the parties are living together or separated, have not been found to predict reabuse. [23] At least one study has found that victim cooperation does not predict recidivism. [145]

Implications for Law Enforcement

Criteria for charges should not be confused with criteria for determining future risk. Abusers cited for misdemeanors are as likely to be dangerous as those charged with felonies. (Research basis: Wide agreement among multiple studies across the nation involving different abuser populations.)

Implications for Prosecutors

Criteria for charges should not be confused with criteria for determining future risk. Abusers charged with misdemeanors are as likely to be dangerous as those charged with felonies. If the offense against a dangerous defendant is not chargeable as a felony, prosecutors should explore the applicability of enhancement statutes for repeat offenses, multiple charges if appropriate, or maximum allowable sentencing recommendations. (Research basis: Wide agreement among multiple studies across the nation involving different abuser populations.)

Implications for Judges

Criteria for charges should not be confused with criteria for determining future risk. Abusers charged with misdemeanors are as likely to be dangerous as those charged with felonies. Although constrained by statute, judges should seek to minimize offender risk to the maximum extent allowable by law. (Research basis: Wide agreement among multiple studies across the nation involving different abuser populations.)

3.18 Do the widely used risk instruments accurately predict reabuse?

All of the common risk instruments in use are insufficient. The best instruments have been found to falsely predict 40 to 43 percent of abusers in both directions. [24, 190] For example, a study of a risk instrument used by police in Berkeley, Calif., found that those abusers classified at highest risk for reoffending did have the highest rate of reoffending but also that the instrument generated 43 percent false positives for predicting reabuse. Those abusers gauged as having the lowest risk of reoffending had 2 percent false negatives. [228]

Implications for Law Enforcement and Prosecutors

Given high base rates of reabusing, the default presumption should be that the defendant is likely to reoffend until proven otherwise. Risk instruments do not significantly improve upon victim perception and basic actuarial data. (Research basis: Not only is there wide agreement among multiple studies but it is also agreed that the same instrument may have different results in different jurisdictions.)

3.19 Which abusers are most likely to try to kill their victims?

Predicting lethality is much more difficult than predicting reabuse and recidivism because, fortunately, it is much rarer. Also, the risk of lethality may increase because of situational circumstances and not because of static abuser characteristics. Nonetheless, researchers have found some key factors that increase the likelihood of homicide or significant injuries.

3.20 How critical is the presence of firearms and other weapons?

According to a CDC study, more female intimate partners are killed by firearms than by all other means combined. [176] Firearms in the household increase the odds of lethal versus nonlethal violence by a factor of 6.1 to 1. Women who were previously threatened or assaulted with a firearm or other weapon are 20 times more likely to be murdered by their abuser than are other women. [25, 142] Prior firearm use includes threats to shoot the victim; cleaning, holding, or loading a gun during an argument; threatening to shoot a pet or a person the victim cares about; and firing a gun during an argument. [17, 191]

A significant Massachusetts study of 31 men imprisoned for murdering their female partners (and willing to talk to researchers) found that almost two-thirds of the guns used by men who shot their partners were illegal because the suspect had a prior abuse assault conviction or a protective order was in effect at the time of the killing. [1]

Implications for Law Enforcement

One of the most crucial steps to prevent lethal violence is to disarm abusers and keep them disarmed. Departments should implement a program to identify firearms in abusers" possession, remove them as soon as legally permissible, and make sure the abuser remains disarmed. If police agencies are involved in firearm licensing, they should aggressively screen for domestic violence, even if it is not discovered initially by inquiries in the FBI"s National Instant Criminal Background Check System (NICS). (Research basis: Multiple studies — national, state and local — support this policy, as do state-by-state correlations between the existence of restrictive gun laws for batterers, state registries to enforce them and lower domestic homicide rates. [217])

Implications for Prosecutors

One of the most crucial steps to prevent lethal violence is to disarm abusers and keep them disarmed. Prosecutors should take all steps possible to have firearms removed by the court as soon as abusers are arrested and obtain guilty verdicts so that federal firearm prohibitions apply (18 U.S.C. § 922(g)(9)). Victims should be advised to obtain protective orders, or the prosecutor should ask the court to order criminal no-contact orders against defendants so that federal firearm prohibitions apply (18 U.S.C. § 922(g)(8)). Prosecutors should collaborate with the U.S. Attorney to refer appropriate firearms violators for federal prosecution, especially where federal penalties are more substantial than state penalties. (Research basis: Although multiple studies document the association between firearms and domestic violence homicides, only one study examined the association between each state"s restrictive gun laws for batterers, state registries to enforce them and lower domestic homicide rates. [217])

Implications for Judges

One of the most crucial steps to prevent lethal violence is to disarm abusers and keep them disarmed. Judges should take all steps possible to have firearms prohibitions enforced and refuse to approve alternative sanctions that preclude federal firearm prohibitions (18 U.S.C. §922(g)(9)). Victims in criminal cases should be advised to obtain protective orders if firearms cannot be removed through the criminal process (18 U.S.C. §922(g)(8)), and vice versa. In 2007, in *Weissenburger* v. *Iowa District Court for Warren County* (No. 47/05-0279, filed October 26, 2007), the Iowa Supreme Court reminded judges they are legally obligated to enforce federal domestic-violence firearm prohibitions, notwithstanding contrary (or silent) state statutes. (Research basis: Multiple studies — national, state and local — support this policy, as do state-by-state correlations between the existence of restrictive gun laws for batterers, state registries to enforce them and lower domestic homicide rates. [217])

3.21 What are other lethality risk markers?

In a national study, other lethality markers that multiply the odds of homicide five times or more over nonfatal abuse have been found to include: (a) threats to kill, 14.9 times more likely; (b) prior attempts to strangle, 9.9 times; (c) forced sex, 7.6 times; (d) escalating physical violence severity over time, 5.2 times; and (e) partner control over the victim"s daily activities, 5.1 times more likely. [25, 142] Research has also found that male abusers are more likely to kill if they are not the fathers of the children in the household. [17, 25, 142] A Chicago study similarly found that death was more likely if the abuser threatened his partner with or used a knife or gun, strangled his partner or grabbed her around her neck, or both partners were drunk. [17]

A series of interviews with 31 men imprisoned for partner murders revealed how quickly abusers turned lethal. Relationships with short courtships were much more likely to end in murder or attempted murder; these relationships were also likelier to end much sooner than those with longer term courtships. Half of the murderers had relationships of no more than three months with the partners they murdered, and almost a third had been involved for only one month. [1]

In terms of female murders of male partners, the research suggests that abused women who killed their partners had experienced more severe and increasing violence over the prior year. They tended to have fewer resources, such as employment or high school education, and were in long-term relationships with their partners at the time. [17]

Implications for Prosecutors

Prosecutors must insist that law enforcement investigators provide them with appropriate information about prior activities, especially those associated with increased risk for lethality. (Research basis: Multiple studies have found similar risk factors for lethality. Although applying risk factors can create false positives, their consideration will avoid false negatives that prove deadly for victims.)

Implications for Judges

For judges to make safe decisions about bail, sentencing or fashioning civil orders, they must insist on appropriate information about abusers" prior activities, including those associated with increased risk for lethality. (Research basis: Multiple studies have found similar risk factors for lethality. Although applying risk factors can create false positives, their consideration will avoid false negatives that prove deadly for victims.)

3.22 What are the risk markers for severe injury?

Medical researchers have looked at severe injuries, those causing victims to seek hospital emergency room treatment. They have found that alcohol abuse, drug use, intermittent employment or recent unemployment, and having less than a high school education distinguish partners of women seeking medical treatment from domestic violence injuries from partners of women seeking treatment for nondomestic violence injuries. In one study, researchers found that 63.7 percent of the abusive partners were alcohol abusers, 36.7 percent abused drugs, a slight majority (51.6 percent) were drinking at the time of the assault, and 14.8 percent admitted to drug use at the time. [144] A similar hospital study found that cocaine use and prior arrests distinguished the violent partners from the nonviolent partners of women admitted to hospitals for treatment of injuries. [95]

Implications for Law Enforcement, Prosecutors and Judges

Prior threats to kill, prior strangulation and sexual assaults, as well as drinking and drugging histories and current use, should be taken very seriously when considering offender dangerousness. (Research basis: Conclusions from repeated studies somewhat overlap, indicating the same or similar risk factors for injury and lethality, including hospital studies of severe injuries of victims not necessarily involved in the criminal justice system.)

4. Victim Characteristics

4.1 Are victim characteristics and actions important factors in assessing the likelihood of abuse?

Victims come in all shapes, sizes, ages and relationships, but these differences are largely irrelevant in terms of their victimization. Victim characteristics — other than gender and age — have generally not been found to be associated with the likelihood of abuse. [23] For example, although many studies have associated pregnancy with increased risk for domestic violence, research suggests that the increased risk is related to the youth of women, not their pregnancy. [219]

Those victims who leave their abusers have been found to be as likely to be reabused as those who remain with them. [141] Those victims who maintain civil restraining orders or criminal no-contact orders against their abusers are as likely to be reabused as those who drop the orders. Only one study [120], comparing women with orders and those without, found that women with permanent as opposed to temporary orders were less likely to have new police-reported domestic violence. However, the researchers in this study excluded violations of the orders themselves, including violations of no-contact or stay-away orders.

Implications for Law Enforcement

Victims face a dilemma — staying or leaving, and securing, maintaining or dropping a protective order may all result in reabuse. Law enforcement officers should assist victims in safeguarding themselves and their children while recognizing their limitations in controlling their abusers. (Research basis: Multiple protective order studies in different jurisdictions over different time periods.)

> **Performance Measure:** A little more than a quarter of both small and large law enforcement agencies require officers to review safety plans with victims, and almost three-quarters of agencies arrange transport of victims to shelters or medical facilities, when needed.

Implications for Prosecutors and Judges

Victims face a dilemma — staying or leaving, and securing, maintaining or dropping a protective order may all result in reabuse. Prosecutors and judges should assist victims in recognizing their limitations in controlling their abusers and safeguarding themselves and their children. Prosecutors must establish effective collaboration with victim advocacy and service agencies in order to refer victims as needed. In addition, prosecutors should advise victims that prosecution, along with civil protective orders, may further victim protection. (Research basis: Findings that protective orders reduce reabuse don't include the order violations themselves, undervaluing the detrimental impact of order violations on victims who have secured them. The research on prosecution efficacy can be found under the question, "Does prosecuting domestic violence offenders deter reabuse?" in the Prosecution Responses section.)

4.2 To what extent do victims engage in alcohol and drug abuse?

Victim abuse of drugs and alcohol is also associated with domestic violence victimization. [153] In the most dramatic findings, victims (or their families) reported in the Memphis night arrest study that 42 percent of victims were drinking or drugging the day of their assault. [19] The New

Mexico fatality review study documented that a third of the female victims had alcohol in their system at the autopsy, with a blood alcohol content of twice the legal limit allowable for driving; a little less than a quarter had drugs in their system. [170] Among women treated in emergency rooms for injuries caused by their abusers, those who suffered from substance abuse were found to have increased risk of violence from partners. However, if the partners" use of alcohol and drugs are controlled for, victim substance abuse is not associated with increased risk of violence. [144] Another hospital study also found that victims who were injured by partners were more likely than other injured women in an emergency room to test positive for substance abuse. [95]

Victim substance abuse has also been found to be associated with abuser use. For example, whereas one in five North Carolina victims reported either being high or binge drinking at the time of abuse, almost three-quarters (72 percent) of these victims were in relationships with men who were high or were binge drinking. [126]

Victim substance abuse has also been identified as a consequence of the ongoing abuse. In other words, victims abuse drugs as a form of self-medication to deal with their abuse trauma. [153]

Implications for Law Enforcement

Victims" abuse of drugs and/or alcohol may make them more vulnerable to continued abuse, requiring greater law enforcement scrutiny or surveillance. Information given to victims should include substance abuse treatment referral information. (Research basis: Multiple single-jurisdiction observational studies of victims as well as findings from a national victim survey of a representative sample of 8,000 women between November 1995 and May 1996.)

Implications for Prosecutors and Judges

Victims" abuse of drugs and/or alcohol may make them more vulnerable to continued abuse. Prosecutors should look at victim vulnerability first and worry about tactical considerations, such as what kind of witness they may make, second. Furthermore, prosecutors should be prepared to file a motion *in limine*, and judges should conduct a hearing, to determine whether to exclude evidence related to a victim"s "bad" character (e.g., substance abuse) that does not directly relate to the abuse incident prosecuted and/or the victim"s ability to perceive or remember the incident. (Research basis: Multiple single-jurisdiction observational studies of victims as well as findings from a national victim survey of a representative sample of 8,000 women between November 1995 and May 1996.)

4.3 Why do some victims behave as they do?

A significant proportion of victims of intimate partner violence and sexual assault suffer from trauma. [3, 153] Studies have found up to 88 percent of battered women in shelters suffer from post-traumatic stress disorder (PTSD). [6] Other studies have found that as many as 72 percent of abuse victims experience depression [212] and 75 percent experience severe anxiety. [76] A meta-analysis across multiple samples of battered women found a weighted mean prevalence of 48 percent for depression and 64 percent for PTSD. [77]

Even victims who do not have PTSD have been found to be severely adversely affected by their abuse. [153] Victims brought to emergency rooms of hospitals, for example, are more socially isolated, have lower self-esteem and have fewer social and financial resources than other women treated for injuries in the same hospital emergency rooms who were not injured by their partners. [95, 153]

Research also suggests that some victims of intimate partner abuse have experienced multifaceted violence that stretches across their life span, beginning in childhood. [143] Such prior victimization is associated with greater risk of more serious (adult) partner violence, particularly **systemic abuse**, which includes physical, sexual and stalking abuse. [153] In short, some of the adult victims who suffer the greatest abuse may be the least able to protect themselves.

Implications for Law Enforcement

Law enforcement officers may find that the most severely traumatized victims behave the least as law enforcement officers expect of them. These victims may be among the least able to cooperate with law enforcement. (Research basis: Multiple victim studies have documented PTSD rates, although many studies obviously seek out samples likely to include the most severely abused victims, such as those in shelters.)

Implications for Prosecutors and Judges

Prosecutors should be prepared to assist and support traumatized victims and/or make appropriate referrals to other service providers. Prosecutors should be prepared to identify, and judges should allow appointment of, expert witnesses if they are needed to educate juries and judges as necessary if a victim"s reaction to trauma appears problematic or counterintuitive. (Research basis: Multiple victim studies have documented PTSD rates, although many studies obviously seek out samples likely to include the most severely abused victims, such as those in shelters.)

4.4   Do male domestic violence victims differ from female victims?

Research on domestic violence victims brought to the attention of law enforcement and the courts find that male victims differ substantially from female victims. [153] First and foremost, male victims of any specific domestic violence incident are more likely than female victims to be **future suspects** for domestic violence. In one of the only studies to track abusers and victims over time, the Charlotte, N.C., law enforcement study found that 41 percent of males who were identified as **victims** and who were involved in new incidents of domestic violence within two years were subsequently identified by police as **suspects**. This compares with only 26.3 percent of females with such role reversals. On the other hand, males identified as suspects were much less likely to be identified later as victims than were female suspects (26 percent vs. 44.4 percent). [68]

Similarly, male victims of domestic violence homicides are much more likely than female victims to have been identified previously as abusers of their eventual killers. [131, 199, 218] Several treatises suggest that the abuse experienced by male victims of female intimates is contextually different than that experienced by women victims of male intimates. [177, 198] Just as male victims differ, so do females convicted of abusing male partners. [162]

Implications for Law Enforcement

Specific incidents of domestic violence may not reveal longer term domestic violence patterns, particularly if the suspect is a female and the victim is a male. Police should acknowledge this and encourage suspects who are more typically victims to report future victimization, notwithstanding their current suspect status. (Research basis: The North Carolina process evaluation of the Charlotte-Mecklenburg police specialized domestic violence unit is unique in looking at subsequent status of victims and suspects in repeat incidents. The study looked at all police complaints involving domestic violence in 2003 that were followed for the next two years, totaling 6,892 domestic violence complaints. The findings are analogous to numerous findings regarding the prior status of male homicide victims as abusers.)

Implications for Prosecutors and Judges

Specific incidents of domestic violence may not reveal longer term domestic violence patterns, particularly if the suspect is a female and the victim is a male. Prosecutors and judges should be sensitive to this fact in charging and recommending sentences for such defendants and in issuing protective orders or fashioning sentences. Typical batterer intervention programs, for example, may not be relevant for abusers engaged in isolated, reactive or defensive behavior. (Research basis: The North Carolina process evaluation of the Charlotte-Mecklenburg police specialized domestic violence unit is unique in looking at subsequent status of victims and suspects in repeat incidents. The study looked at all police complaints involving domestic violence in 2003 followed for the next two years, totaling 6,892 domestic violence complaints in all. The findings are analogous to numerous findings regarding the prior status of male homicide victims as abusers. The analysis of batterer programs for court-referred female defendants is based on limited qualitative research that focused on content relevance based on defendant abuse histories.)

5. Law Enforcement Responses

5.1 Are specialized law enforcement domestic violence units effective in responding to domestic violence?

Performance Measure: A total of 11 percent of police departments have specialized domestic violence units, according to a national survey of a representative sample of 14,000 law enforcement agencies. Most domestic violence units work within investigative units and are most common in larger departments. A majority of departments (56 percent) with 100 or more officers have specialized domestic violence units. Although only 4 percent of departments maintain domestic violence information on their Web sites, three-quarters of those departments also have specialized domestic violence units. [213] (Research basis: A representative sample drawn from 14,000 law enforcement agencies across the nation.)

5.2 Do they influence prosecutions and convictions of abuse suspects?

Specialized domestic violence units, emphasizing repeat victim contact and evidence gathering, have been shown to significantly increase the likelihood of prosecution, conviction and sentencing. [130] Specialized domestic violence units are generally associated with more extensive inquiries by police department call takers — asking if weapons are involved, advising callers to stay on the line until police arrive, asking if children are present, whether the suspect uses drugs/alcohol, whether restraining orders are in effect, and whether the suspect is on probation or parole. [213] Domestic violence units are also more likely to amass evidence to turn over to prosecutors. The specialized unit in Mecklenburg County, Charlotte, N.C., collected evidence in 61.8 percent of its cases, compared to only 12.5 percent of cases collected by patrol officers. In addition, whereas 30 percent of victims handled by regular patrols declined to prosecute, only 8 percent of victims handled by the specialized unit declined to prosecute. [68]

5.3 Do they influence victim behavior?

Specialized police response is more likely to see victims leave their abusers sooner — within four months, compared to an average of 14 months for victims not receiving specialized police response. Specialized police response also results in higher victim reporting of reabuse. Finally, victims handled by specialized police response are more likely to secure protective orders against their abusers. [130] Specialized police services such as serving protective orders and assisting in safety planning also influence victim behavior. By contrast, victim services alone have not been found to be associated with victims leaving abusers, although this may also be due to the quality of the victim services studied. [172, 220]

5.4 Do they reduce reabuse?

An early study of a specialized detective unit in Dade County, Fla., found that it did not affect reabuse rates. [174] However, the detective unit focused on referring parties to counseling. Subsequently, specialized units have been found to be more effective: Victims self-report significantly less reabuse but are more likely to report the reabuse they do suffer. [130] Another study found that specialized responses reduce "personal harm" but not nonpersonal harm, such as property damage. The positive effect may be tied to the safety planning offered to victims. [68] By contrast, research found that victim services alone are not associated with increased victim safety. [172, 220] Research in New York City among victims in public housing suggest that specific crime prevention training, as opposed to general victim counseling, may be associated more closely with reduced subsequent victimization. [37]

In North Carolina, 29 percent of the abusers handled by the specialized domestic violence unit had at least one subsequent domestic violence offense during a two-year follow-up period, compared to 37 percent of abusers handled solely by patrol units. This reduced rate was obtained even though the specialized unit handled more serious cases and offenders with more prior offenses. The odds ratio on reoffending for suspects handled by domestic violence units was nearly half that for suspects not handled by these units. Domestic violence suspects who reabused also reabused less often, averaging 0.46 new assaults compared to 0.62. The difference is statistically significant but, because fewer units" abusers reabused, the actual difference in the number of new incidents for just those abusers who reabused was less (1.59 vs. 1.67), not reaching statistical significance. [68]

5.5 Do they increase victim satisfaction?

Victim satisfaction with the criminal justice system is not associated with whether the victim received advocacy per se, but rather with concrete law enforcement activities such as issuance of a warrant against absent abusers or assistance in obtaining protective orders. [220] Similarly, the NVAWS found that stalking victims whose stalkers were arrested were significantly more likely to be satisfied with the police response than those in situations where no arrest was made (76 percent vs. 42 percent). [208]

Studies of victim dissatisfaction generally focus on four major themes: (1) adverse personal outcomes (victim arrested, child protection agency called), (2) the police "made assumptions or did not listen," (3) the police took sides (against her), and (4) nothing happened (a strong court sanction was absent). [151]

Implications for Law Enforcement

The single, most appreciated service that officers can deliver to the greatest number of victims is the arrest of their abusers. Specialized domestic violence law enforcement units that focus on arrests can enhance the likelihood of successful prosecution and increase victim satisfaction and safety. (Research basis: Although specific studies of specialized domestic violence law enforcement units are few, the activities conducted by these units have been more widely studied and supported by extensive research.)

5.6 Should law enforcement agencies participate in coordinated community responses?

A number of jurisdictions have endeavored to create what have been called ***coordinated community responses***, composed of multiple criminal justice and social service agencies that respond to domestic violence. This approach may exert a positive impact on both case processing and reabuse, according to initial research. [118] For example, both arrests and successful prosecutions increased in several Minnesota jurisdictions with the creation of coordinated community responses involving law enforcement. [69] Other studies have found similar promising results [118], although more is required than participation in multidisciplinary task forces for communities to create effective coordinated responses. [227] Personnel of relatively autonomous organizations (both public and private) cannot be presumed to have the organizational capacity or the willingness among their personnel to truly collaborate. [73]

Performance Measure: A total of 65 percent of police departments have established partnerships with community-based victim advocacy groups, according to a national survey of 14,000 police departments. [213] (Research basis: A representative sample drawn from 14,000 law enforcement agencies across the nation.)

5.7 Does domestic violence training improve law enforcement responses to victims?

Several studies suggest that general domestic violence training for law enforcement officers does not necessarily change attitudes toward domestic violence or, more important, change police behavior in terms of arrests of abusers or responses to domestic violence incidents. Although knowing a department's policy regarding domestic violence arrest preference increases the likelihood that officers will arrest alleged domestic violence suspects, the amount of domestic violence training received does not. [59, 65, 197] Research suggests that domestic violence arrest decisions are influenced more by an officer's assessment of the legal variables involved than by his or her attitudes. [117] At least one study suggests that failure of police managers to hold police officers accountable for failure to arrest in contravention of statutory requirements is responsible for their poor performance, not their lack of training. [187]

Implications for Law Enforcement

Clear policy pronouncements from the top administration may be more likely to change officer responses to domestic violence than is general domestic violence training aimed at education and attitude change. (Research basis: There is limited research in this area.)

Performance Measure: A survey of a sample of law enforcement departments across the nation finds that three-quarters have written domestic violence policies in place. Most have been in place for six years or longer. A large majority of departments (88 percent) require officers to complete incident reports for all domestic violence calls they are dispatched to, regardless of outcome. Almost two-thirds of departments (63 percent) require officers to fill out a supplemental form for domestic violence, and most require written justification when no arrest is made (68 percent) or when there is a dual arrest (86 percent). [213] (Research basis: A representative sample drawn from 14,000 law enforcement agencies across the nation.)

6. Prosecution Responses

6.1 What is the current level of domestic violence prosecution across the country?

Although there remain wide disparities in the prosecution of domestic violence cases from one jurisdiction to another, routine prosecution of domestic violence arrests is no longer exceptional or rare. In fact, prosecutors who automatically dismiss or *nolle prosse* almost all domestic violence cases may be increasingly rare and exceptional.

A total of 120 studies from over 170 mostly urban jurisdictions in 44 states and the District of Columbia (and a few foreign countries) of intimate-partner prosecutions between 1973 and 2006 [71] found the average arrest prosecution rate was 63.8 percent, ranging from a low of 4.6 percent of 802 arrests in Milwaukee in 1988-1989 to 94 percent of 3,662 arrests in Cincinnati in 1993-1996. The rate of offense prosecution was lower, with an average of 27.4 percent, ranging from a low of 2.6 percent for more than 5,000 offenses in Detroit in 1983 to 72.5 percent for more than 5,000 offenses reported in Boulder County, Colo., in 2003-2005.

Several studies demonstrate that domestic violence prosecutions can be routine across entire states, notwithstanding demographic, prosecution and law enforcement variations across counties and localities. A study of 15,000 protective order violations across Massachusetts between 1992 and 1995 found that 60 percent were prosecuted in total. [10] A study of 4,351 felony domestic violence prosecutions in South Carolina between 1996 and 2000 found a 46 percent prosecution rate. [21] Similarly, a study of 238,000 misdemeanor domestic violence charges between 1997 and 2002 in North Carolina found a prosecution rate of 47 percent. [16]

Jurisdictions with specialized domestic violence prosecution programs generally boast higher rates. A study of San Diego"s City Attorney"s Office documented that prosecutors prosecuted 70 percent of cases brought by police. Similarly, specialized prosecutors in Omaha, Neb., prosecuted 88 percent of all police domestic violence arrests. In several of these sites, comparisons before and after implementation of the specialized prosecution program found marked increases in prosecutions. In Everett, Wash., dismissals dropped from 79 percent to 29 percent, and in Klamath Falls, Ore., they dropped from 47 percent to 14 percent. [196]

On the other hand, not all domestic violence cases are equally likely to be prosecuted. The research indicates that prosecutions of intimate-partner stalking [160] and intimate-partner sexual assault [161] are rare. The research also reflects very low arrest rates for these offenses.

Implications for Prosecutors

Prosecutors who fail to prosecute the **majority** of domestic violence arrests made by police should examine their practices, policies and priorities to determine why they are prosecuting fewer domestic violence arrests than their peers around the country. (Research basis: Multiple studies, including at least three statewide studies.)

6.2 Can most domestic violence arrest cases be successfully prosecuted in court?

Not all cases filed by prosecutors go to trial. As with most offenses, most domestic violence prosecutions are disposed of as a result of plea and sentencing negotiations. Of those that go to trial, not all prosecutions result in convictions. However, studies indicate that, in general, domestic violence prosecutions that go to trial routinely result in court convictions. "Not guilty" findings are rare. Studies document findings that range from a high of only 5.0 percent in Ohio [11], to 2.7 percent in Massachusetts [23], to a low of 1.6 percent in North Carolina. [68] A study of felony domestic violence prosecutions in Brooklyn, N.Y., found a similarly low "not guilty" rate of only 2 percent. [164]

For most domestic violence cases that do not go to trial, an analysis of 85 domestic violence prosecution studies found an overall conviction rate of 35 percent, ranging from a low of 8.1 percent of 37 cases prosecuted in Milwaukee between 1988 and 1989 to a high of 90.1 percent of 229 cases in Brooklyn, N.Y., prosecuted in 1997. If one very large study of 123,507 Maryland prosecutions from 1993 to 2003 is removed, the average conviction rate increases to almost half, 47.7 percent. [71] In three statewide prosecution studies of tens of thousands of domestic violence cases, similar conviction rates ranged from one-third in North Carolina to more than one-half in South Carolina. [16, 21]

Jurisdictions with specialized domestic violence prosecution programs boast higher rates: 96 percent in San Diego, 85 percent in Omaha, Neb., 78 percent in Klamath Falls, Ore., and 55 percent in Everett, Wash. The latter rate was the lowest because prosecutors maintained a diversion program that siphoned off 22 percent of the cases prosecuted. [196]

As important, multiple studies also find that convictions can be consistently obtained that include the most intrusive disposition, sentences of incarceration. For example, in the three statewide domestic violence prosecution studies, 12.6 percent of the Massachusetts [10] and 20 percent of the North Carolina [16] misdemeanant domestic violence defendants prosecuted were sentenced to incarceration. In South Carolina, almost half (45 percent) of felony domestic violence defendants prosecuted were sentenced to prison. [21] In Brooklyn Felony Domestic Violence Court, 80 to 85 percent of all convicted offenders were sentenced to incarceration consistently during the study period of 1996 through 2000. [164] Although the latter single court incarceration rate may have been the result of a singular effort on the part of prosecutors and others, the statewide rates include multiple prosecutors across each state.

Many other disparate court studies document incarceration rates ranging from 76 percent to 21 percent: 76 percent in Klamath Falls, Ore. [196]; 70 percent in Cincinnati, Ohio, with the largest number incarcerated between 150 and 180 days [11]; 56 percent in Everett, Wash. [196]; 52 percent in Omaha, Neb. [196]; 39 percent in the Bronx, N.Y. [185]; 35 percent in Brooklyn, N.Y. [31]; 30 percent in Milwaukee [39]; 23 percent in Chicago (including time jailed pending prosecution) [107]; 22.5 percent in Quincy, Mass. [23]; and 21 percent in San Diego, Calif. [196] A study of intimate-partner arrests across three states — Connecticut, Idaho and Virginia — found similarly intrusive dispositions, with three-quarters of those convicted, incarcerated, sentenced to probation or fined. [117]

Implications for Prosecutors

The research suggests that domestic violence cases can be successfully prosecuted at trial, and a large proportion of cases (and most cases in some jurisdictions) can be disposed of before trial, even without removing incarceration as an outcome. (Research basis: Multiple studies in disparate jurisdictions for both felony and misdemeanor domestic violence prosecutions.)

> **Performance Measure:** Norfolk County, Mass., prosecutors brought 505 charges arising out of 342 domestic violence incidents studied, compared to 531

charges initially filed by arresting police departments, a dropoff of only 5 percent. Prosecutors enhanced charges of felony assault from 14.1 percent filed by police to 23.8 percent. Prosecutors proceeded to *nolle prosequi* in 18.5 percent of the cases and asked that an additional 10 percent be dismissed in court. With the exception of 2.5 percent of arrests that resulted in not-guilty findings, the remaining defendants were either found guilty after trial or admitted to sufficient facts for a finding of guilty (although judges initially allowed 25 percent of the cases to be conditionally continued without imposition of a guilty finding). (Research basis: The studies followed 342 arrests that occurred within Eastern Norfolk County and followed them as long as 10 years. [23, 138])

6.3 Will aggressive prosecutions or sentences increase the demand for trials?

A study of four prosecution programs in four states where prosecutors specifically adopted (what they claimed to be) "no drop" prosecution policies (and in fact proceeded with the majority of all cases brought by law enforcement) found that trial rates ranged from a high of 13 percent to just 1 percent. Further research has suggested that the highest rates would recede once the aggressive prosecution programs were more established. In San Diego, which had adopted a no-drop policy a decade earlier, only 2 percent of the cases subsequently went to trial. [196] Furthermore, in these no-drop jurisdictions, sentencing included incarceration in 21 to 76 percent of the four jurisdictions. [196]

Implications for Prosecutors

Increased domestic violence prosecutions may not result in a dramatically increased proportion of trials, although there may be a transitory increase as defenders test prosecution resolve. (Research basis: Although implications are based on only one study, the study looked at four different no-drop prosecution programs in four states.)

Implications for Judges

Judicial administrators can rest assured that aggressive domestic violence prosecution will **not** result in dramatically increased and sustained demand for jury or bench trials. (Research basis: Although implications are based on one study, the study looked at four different no-drop prosecution programs in four states.)

6.4 Do victims want their abusers prosecuted?

If asked to declare publicly in court in front of their abusers, victims may express ambivalence about the prosecution and/or sentencing of their abusers. However, in interviews with researchers, often a majority of victims support domestic violence prosecutions and sentencing, especially mandatory referral to batterer programs. In a Chicago misdemeanor court study, approximately two-thirds of victims (67.6 percent) reported that they wanted their abusers to be prosecuted **and** jailed. [107] A study of four prosecution programs in California, Washington, Oregon and Nebraska, found that three-quarters (76 percent) of the victims interviewed wanted their abusers arrested, and 55 percent want them prosecuted. Furthermore, 59 percent expressed satisfaction with the outcome, and 67 percent expressed satisfaction with the judge, once the cases were prosecuted. [196]

Even when the majority of victims oppose prosecution, after trial they may change their minds. In the Quincy arrest study, only 46.8 percent wanted their abusers to be prosecuted as charged or wanted more serious charges filed. However, after trial, 53.4 percent said the court experience gave them a "sense of control," 36.9 percent said it motivated them to end the relationship with their abuser, and 38.8 percent said it "made them safer." Most victims (71 percent) who did not want the case to go to court expressed satisfaction after the trial. [23] Similarly, a study of four specialized prosecution programs in four different states found that although 45 percent did not want their cases prosecuted, once they were prosecuted, only 14 percent tried to stop the prosecutors and only 4 percent said they wanted the court to let the defendant go. About three-quarters (72.1 percent) reported that they wanted the defendant jailed and/or ordered into treatment (79 percent). Sixty-four percent (64 percent) expressed satisfaction with the prosecution, another 9 percent were neutral, and only 27 percent were dissatisfied. Most (85 percent) reported that they felt the prosecution was helpful. [196]

Implications for Prosecutors

Prosecutors should not allow victim opposition to automatically stop them from prosecuting cases. If prosecutors find that the overwhelming majority of victims consistently oppose prosecution, they should examine both their and law enforcement"s interaction with victims to increase support of prosecution from victims that is more in line with that found across the rest of the country. (Research basis: Numerous studies from disparate jurisdictions.)

Implications for Judges

Judges should not assume that allowing cases to proceed over victim objections will necessarily embitter victims or jeopardize their safety. (Research basis: Numerous studies from disparate jurisdictions on victim attitudes toward prosecution, and several studies on court sentencing.)

6.5 Why do a minority of victims oppose prosecution?

Although studies have found multiple reasons for victim opposition to prosecution, fear is among the leading reasons expressed by victims. Fear of the abuser is first and foremost, followed by fear of testifying in court.

A study of five jurisdictions in three states found that victims across all sites reported that fear of defendant retaliation was their most common barrier to participation with prosecutors. [103] Even in a Chicago study where the majority of Chicago victims wanted their abusers prosecuted, fear was the biggest factor for those who opposed prosecution. A quarter of victims opposing prosecution reported being specifically threatened by their abusers against prosecution. Others expressed fear that their abusers would become more violent. In addition to fear, almost half who wanted the prosecution to be dropped thought it wouldn"t make any difference. About a third of the victims opposed prosecution because they depended on their abusers for housing. [107]

In addition to fear of the abuser, an Ohio study found that more victims were actually more afraid of testifying in court than they were of the defendant or compromising their relationship with the defendant. Specifically, victims expressed fear that the prosecutors would not prepare them adequately to testify. They were also concerned that the defendant might not be found guilty. [11]

Implications for Prosecutors

To increase victim cooperation and participation in prosecution, prosecutors must address victim fears of reabuse *and* of testifying in court. (Research basis: Several victim studies in different jurisdictions.)

6.6 Is victim fear of prosecution well founded?

Victim fear of their abusers appears to be well founded. Multiple prosecution and arrest studies broadly concur that abusers who come to the attention of the criminal justice system who reabuse are likely to do so sooner rather than later. In the Quincy court study, about 40 percent of the arrested abusers reabused their victims within one year. Forty-four percent did so **before** the study arrest was prosecuted in court. The average case took about six months from arraignment to prosecution. [23] Similarly, in a Cook County study, 30 percent of the defendants were rearrested within six months of their study arrest, and half of the arrests were for a new domestic violence offense. The average rearrest time was only 29 days after initial arrest. In addition, in almost half of the cases (45.9 percent), the defendants tried to talk the female victims out of testifying. Moreover, 29.1 percent of these defendants stalked their victims before the trial, and 8.7 percent specifically threatened them. [107] An Indianapolis prosecution study found that almost a quarter of the defendants reabused their victims before the pending trial. [67]

In the Brooklyn Specialized Felony Domestic Violence Court — where cases took 6.5 to 7.0 months, on average, to be disposed — 51 percent of defendants charged with domestic felonies (other than violation of protective orders) were rearrested before disposition; 14 percent were arrested for a crime of violence; and 16 percent were arrested for violation of a protection order. Among those charged with order violations — a felony in New York — the rearrest rate was 47 percent, including 37 percent for violating the protective order again. [164]

Although these studies do not demonstrate that prosecution causes reabuse, they indicate that pending prosecution by itself may not deter recidivist abusers.

Implications for Prosecutors and Judges

Prosecutors must gauge defendant risk pending trial and take appropriate measures to address it in order to protect victims and to successfully prosecute the case. Judges should insist that police and prosecutors document and inform the court if defendants reabuse, threaten or intimate victims while cases are pending so that possible additional charges can be filed and subsequent absences of victims who are too fearful to testify in court can be justified, allowing for substitute hearsay testimony. The equitable doctrine of forfeiture, affirmed in *Davis* v. *Washington*, 126 S. Ct. 2266, 2280 (2006), precludes a defendant from using his right to confrontation to bar the admission of a victim"s statements when his wrongdoing caused her unavailability at trial. (Research basis: Rapid reabuse rates are documented in multiple studies from disparate jurisdictions. Research on the impact of specific prosecution practices is rare. Victim fear is documented in several victim studies in different jurisdictions.)

6.7 Can prosecutors increase victim cooperation?

Although victims most commonly reported fear of retaliation as a barrier to their participation in prosecution, a three-state study found that the fear was reduced at sites with specialized prosecution programs, increased victim advocacy and specialized domestic violence courts. [103] These specialized response programs generally include fast-track scheduling, reducing victim vulnerability pending trial, increased victim contact pending trial, and victim-friendly proceedings that remove, as much as possible, victim involvement to proceed with prosecution. These measures contrast with those used in some jurisdictions, in which studies indicate some prosecutors treat victims like civil claimants. In a large 45-county study of upstate New York domestic violence prosecutions, researchers found that half of the prosecutors required victims to sign complaints in order to file charges. (On the other hand, two-thirds required victims to sign affidavits to confirm their interest in having charges withdrawn.) [227]

There is more research on what not to do than on what works. Specific studies suggest that the more prosecution-related burdens are placed on victims, the less likely they are to cooperate. In Milwaukee, a study found the majority of cases were dismissed when victims were required to attend a charging conference within days of the arrest of their abusers. However, absolved of this responsibility, Milwaukee prosecution rates increased from 20 percent to 60 percent. [38] In a similar vein, a comparison of protective order violation prosecutions across Massachusetts found a 66 percent dismissal rate when prosecutors routinely provided and encouraged victims to sign waivers of prosecution forms (often in front of defendants), compared to a 33-percent dismissal rate in an adjacent county in which victims were not provided this alternative. [10]

Some prosecutors are better at maintaining contact with victims than others. The Ohio court study found that the majority of victims never received rudimentary information from prosecutors before trial, including court dates. In almost 90 percent of the court cases, prosecutors never spoke with the victim on the phone and, in more than half of the cases (52 percent), never met with them before the trial date. When they did meet, it typically was for no more than a few minutes. [11] The importance of prosecutor-victim contact is underscored by a Toronto study that found if the victim met with a victim/witness representative, victim cooperation increased by a factor of 3.3. [43] In the Ohio court study, the strongest predictor of a guilty verdict in domestic violence misdemeanor cases was how many times the prosecutors met with the victim before trial. [11]

A limited number of studies that looked at the role of court-based victim advocates suggest that they may help in this regard. The studies found that victims appreciated contact with victim advocates/liaisons and reported a high degree of satisfaction. In the Quincy study, 81 percent of the victims reported satisfaction with the time they spent with victim advocates, and three-quarters (77 percent) said they would talk to the advocate again if a similar incident recurred. [23] Chicago domestic violence victims who had contact with victim advocates reported more satisfaction with the proceedings than those who had no contact. However, the same study reported that advocates" contact with victims did not make the victims more likely to come to court. [107]

The seeds for victim contact may be planted before the case even reaches prosecutors. A Portland, Ore., police study found that the following police activities significantly correlated with increased prosecution: (1) police contacted victims, (2) victim accepted services, (3) police provided victims with prosecution information, (4) police helped set up victim appointments with prosecutors, and (5) police helped victims obtain restraining orders and served the orders. [130]

Implications for Prosecutors

Victim cooperation can be enhanced if prosecutors can address victim fear of their abusers as well as their fear around being involved in subsequent legal proceedings. Pretrial conditions or detention and/or speedy trial dates may address victim fear and minimize actions required of victims, and sensitivity to victim needs may address their fear of court proceedings. The quality of police contact with victims may also be important for subsequent successful prosecution. (Research basis: Multiple studies and victim interviews in multiple studies.)

> **Performance Measure:** Over 80 percent of victims were contacted by a prosecutor advocate in the Quincy court arrest and prosecution study; 42 percent of

the victims had 45 minutes or more with an advocate, and the remainder had less time with one. [23]

6.8 Should prosecutors follow victim preferences when prosecuting offenders?

Although victim perceptions of the dangerousness of suspects have been found to be good predictors of subsequent revictimization [23, 112, 113], victim preferences on how the case should be prosecuted are not good predictors. The victims in the Quincy study who wanted the charges dropped were as likely to be revictimized (51 vs. 48 percent after one year) as those who did not want the charges dropped. [23] Similarly, studies in New York found that victim cooperation with prosecutors did not predict recidivism. In other words, if prosecutors proceeded with uncooperative victims, these victims were no more or less likely to be revictimized than victims who cooperated with prosecutors. [145]

Implications for Prosecutors

Although prosecutors should listen to victims, they should explain to victims (and, as important, to defendants) that the decision to prosecute cannot be based solely on victims" preferences.

6.9 What evidence is typically available to prosecute domestic violence cases?

One of the challenges domestic violence prosecutors face is the lack of evidence accompanying their cases. A study of domestic violence across Rhode Island in 2002, based on 6,200 police incident reports involving adult victims under 50 years of age, found the following evidence reported in cases: victim photos (17 percent), crime scene photos (16 percent), suspect photos (3 percent), physical evidence (8 percent) and weapons collected (11 percent), medical reports (9.4 percent), witnesses" interviews (37 percent: adults 24 percent, children 12 percent), suspect statements (18 percent) and signed victim statements (53 percent). [138] The Rhode Island data are not unique.

In the Mecklenburg County, N.C., study, researchers found that presentation of physical evidence to the special domestic violence prosecution unit was rare. Photos were available in only 15 percent of the cases submitted by patrol officers and only 30.5 percent of cases submitted by the police department"s specialized domestic violence unit. Medical evidence was available in less than 10 percent of the patrol cases and 34 percent of the special-unit cases, which selected out the more serious cases such as those involving injuries. Given the fact that most domestic violence incidents occur in private, it is not surprising that witnesses were available in only 16 percent of the patrol cases and 19 percent of the special-unit cases. [68] Similarly, the Ohio court study found that photos of injuries and damages were available in only 14.3 percent of the cases, 911 tapes in only 2.2 percent, medical records in 1.7 percent, eyewitness testimony in only 1.6 percent, and police officer testimony in only 6.7 percent of the cases. [11]

One reason medical evidence may be limited is because of medical staff"s poor handwriting. A study found that in records of medical visits containing indications of abuse or injury, one-third of the notes written by the doctors or nurses contained vital information that was illegible. [127]

Implications for Prosecutors

Especially in light of *Crawford v. Washington*, 541 U.S. 36 (2004), prosecutors must work with law enforcement to gather as much evidence as possible and accurately identify all potential witnesses and ways to contact them, or identify third parties who will remain in touch with them. Vital witnesses may include third parties whom victims spoke to at the time of the incident. Statements that victims make to third parties are generally nontestimonial and therefore admissible at trial. Children may also be potential witnesses. The presence of children may also allow prosecutors to file additional charges against abusers for endangering the welfare of the child or allow them to file a similar charge that can go forward, even if the original charges cannot. (Research basis: Few studies review domestic violence evidence as a separate issue; these studies suggest that evidence collection can be dramatically improved.)

Consequently, prosecutors must rely on victims. In the Ohio court study, victim testimony was the evidence most frequently relied upon by prosecutors, available in 48 percent of the 2,952 domestic violence cases studied. [11] In Rhode Island, victims provided signed statements in 53 percent of the incident reports. [139] A Canadian study of a Toronto Domestic Violence Court found that, although having witnesses or corroborating evidence does not increase the likelihood of prosecution, if the victim cooperates, the odds of prosecution increase by a factor of 8, compared to cases in which the victim does not cooperate. [43] In Chicago, prosecutors achieved a 73-percent conviction rate for domestic violence cases when the victim showed up in court, and significantly less (only 23 percent) when they did not show. [107]

Generally, lack of cooperative or available victims is cited as the prime reason prosecutors drop or dismiss domestic violence cases. In the Quincy, Mass., arrest study, a quarter of the arrested abusers were not prosecuted by the district attorney"s office. When indicated in the court file, the most common reason given was "victim denies abuse" (18.8 percent), married victims invoked their marital privilege not to testify against their husband suspects (12.9 percent), or the victim could not be located (10.6 percent). [23] In the large Ohio study, 70.5 percent of cases were dismissed because of victim "unavailability/failure to attend." [11] In another Ohio study, in Toledo, analysis of a sample derived from 1,982 misdemeanor domestic violence cases before the municipal court found that 70 percent of dismissed cases were dismissed because the "victim failed to appear." [216] In North Carolina, victim opposition was reported as the key factor in reducing the likelihood of prosecution. [119]

Implications for Law Enforcement

Prosecutors must work with local law enforcement to identify and obtain critical evidence whenever it is available, including information on how to locate and contact victims and other potential witnesses. (Research basis: Several large court and statewide studies in disparate jurisdictions indicate law enforcement"s failure to provide available evidence.)

6.10 Can cases be successfully prosecuted without the victim?

Despite the fact that most prosecutors see the lack of victim cooperation as the reason why domestic violence prosecutions cannot proceed, both individual-jurisdiction and comparative studies clearly suggest that either lack of victim cooperation is exaggerated or victims are not the key variable in successful prosecution programs.

A study of almost 100 domestic violence trials in San Diego found that uniformly high conviction rates were obtained independent of victim or defendant statements, witness testimony and corroborating evidence. In fact, outcomes were also independent of whether the victim testified for the prosecution or for the defense. [196]

Other comparative studies consistently found that the determination of prosecutors rather than the availability of victims or other evidence accounted for varying rates of prosecution. For example, in the three statewide examinations of tens of thousands of domestic violence prosecutions, researchers documented widely varying rates of prosecution across equivalent counties. In Massachusetts, county prosecution rates ranged from 82 percent to 25 percent. [10] In South Carolina, prosecution rates varied from 69 percent to 22 percent from one prosecution district to another. [21] Similarly, in North Carolina, prosecution rates ranged from 57 percent to 21 percent in specific prosecution districts. [16] Although some of the counties or prosecutorial districts differed in terms of demographics and population density, even among those that did not, prosecution rates varied greatly. In fact, in South Carolina, after the study was published in the newspaper and the state"s attorney general ordered prosecutors to prosecute all cases, the statewide dismissal rate dropped by 29 percent the next month. [20]

Studies confirm that jurisdictions with specialized domestic violence prosecution programs generally support the highest rates of successful prosecution. [196] These specialized programs apparently create their own momentum. For example, they either help create or are associated with courts that create expedited domestic violence dockets. As a result of the specialized prosecution in San Diego, processing time for domestic violence cases decreased to 32 days, with almost half of the defendants (46 percent) pleading at the arraignment. Similarly, in Everett, Wash., time to trial was 80 days, and in Omaha, Neb., it was 43 days. Shortened trial times reduce both victim vulnerability to threats and chances of reconciling with the abuser pending trial. In both San Diego and Everett, bails were regularly set at $10,000 per domestic violence charge (with no cash alternative in the latter location). As a result, for defendants unable to raise bail, the incentive is to plead guilty to get *out* of jail.

In these jurisdictions, researchers found that evidence (eyewitnesses, photos, admissions, excited utterances, medical evidence and physical evidence) was *not* uniformly the most powerful predictor of prosecutors" decisions to proceed without victims and was not significantly associated with the decision to prosecute at all in Klamath Falls, Ore. [196]

Supporting the contention that prosecutorial determination is a powerful predictor of prosecutorial success, the Ohio court study found that increased time the prosecutor spent with victims while preparing the case was positively associated with successful prosecution, and large prosecution caseloads were negatively associated with successful outcomes. The availability of evidence (911 tapes, photographs, medical records and police testimony) was *not* associated with the likelihood of a conviction. Researchers did not suggest that only victims with strong cases self-selected to approach prosecutors. [11]

Implications for Prosecutors

Lack of evidence may be more likely to deter prosecutors from going forward than deterring juries from convicting defendants or deterring defendants from pleading guilty. (Research basis: Multiple studies have found prosecutors able to consistently achieve high conviction rates, notwithstanding consistently limited evidence. The analysis of San Diego trials specifically suggests that convictions may be obtained with varying types of evidence, notwithstanding absence of types of other evidence, including that from victims.)

Implications for Prosecutors

Parity should exist between prosecutors and defenders as well as between prosecutors and crimes to be prosecuted. In the Ohio study, where large prosecution caseloads were associated with unsuccessful domestic violence prosecution, the court had 31 public defenders but only 18 prosecutors. (Research basis: Only one study.)

6.11 Can successful prosecutions be increased?

There have been multiple studies of specific prosecution efforts to significantly increase prosecution by adopting no-drop policies. Although the concept of a no-drop policy has proven elastic, the success of these programs in significantly increasing prosecution has been demonstrated in multiple jurisdictions. In the Queens Borough of New York City, prosecutors increased convictions from 24 to 60 percent. Research suggests that much of the increase was the result of increased follow-up with victims, and prosecutor"s improved linkage with police (e.g., monitoring the same case log, and asking whether each of eight evidentiary items were covered in police incident reports, including photos and witness, victim and suspect statements). [159] A study of domestic violence prosecutions in two other states similarly found greatly increased conviction rates as a result of adopting no-drop policies accompanied by increased coordination with police. [196]

A study of specialized prosecution programs in Oregon and Washington that instituted no-drop policies found that increased use of evidence-based prosecution dramatically increased conviction rates, reduced processing time and initially increased trials. Dismissal rates more than halved in Everett, Wash., from 79 to 29 percent, and guilty findings increased from 10 to 53 percent (although diversion increased from 2 to 22 percent), whereas processing time declined from 109 days to 80 days. Trials increased from 1 percent to 10 percent. Conviction rates at trial were 80 percent. In Klamath Falls, Ore., only 10 to 20 percent of cases were screened out by prosecutors. Dismissals dropped from 47 to 14 percent, and convictions rose from 47 to 86 percent after introduction of evidence-based prosecution. Unlike in Everett, diverted cases dropped from 6 percent to none. Trials rose from 1 percent to 13 percent, and prosecutors won 63 percent of them. [196]

6.12 What does adoption of no-drop policies actually mean?

The most comprehensive study of model no-drop prosecution programs, including several that received large Justice Department grants, found that no-drop policies meant that approximately 30 percent of cases brought by police were screened out, but most of the remaining cases proceeded. Even when victims were not present at the time of trial, prosecutors typically were still able to proceed with 60 to 70 percent of the cases. [196]

Implications for Prosecutors

Although *Crawford* v. *Washington* further inhibits domestic violence prosecutors, the dramatic increase in successful prosecutions, with implementation of specialized domestic violence prosecution programs, suggests that most prosecutors should be able to significantly increase successful prosecutions but perhaps not as much as documented in these pre-*Crawford* studies. (Research basis: Multiple studies in disparate jurisdictions before the U.S. Supreme Court decided *Crawford*.)

6.13 What kind of dispositions do most suspects receive?

Just as prosecution rates vary widely, so does sentencing of domestic violence perpetrators, even though the vast majority of domestic violence defendants are prosecuted for misdemeanor assaults. Disparate studies from various jurisdictions illustrate some of the variety of sentences imposed.

In Quincy, where almost three-quarters of the suspects were charged with some form of assault and/or battery, about one-quarter of the defendants were diverted after a plea to sufficient facts, another quarter were sentenced to probation, and a little over one-tenth were imprisoned. The remainder defaulted or had their cases filed. [23] In Ohio, of those found guilty, almost 70 percent were incarcerated. The largest number were incarcerated between 30 and 45 days, but 18.8 percent were incarcerated for 150 to 180 days. A little more than 60 percent of those found guilty were placed under probation supervision. The largest number of defendants (30.8 percent) were incarcerated between 360 and 499 days. [11] In the Brooklyn misdemeanor domestic violence court study of 9,157 cases in 2002, of those defendants pleading or found guilty, 51 percent received a conditional discharge, 35 percent received a jail sentence, 7 percent received probation, 5 percent were ordered to complete community service and 1 percent were fined. [31] In Milwaukee, in the mid-1990s, out of 669 sample cases prosecutors accepted for prosecution, 30 percent were convicted with a jail sentence, and a little less than one-quarter were sentenced to probation. [39] In Chicago, a little less than one-third of the defendants were given conditional discharges, 24 percent were placed on probation or under court supervision and 23 percent received a jail sentence (including time served pending trial). [107] A study of more than 1,000 domestic violence arrests across three states (Connecticut, Idaho and Virginia) found that, of those convicted, three-quarters were incarcerated, sentenced to probation and/or fined. A little less than half (46.7 percent) were ordered into either anger management or batterer programs. [117]

A study of three domestic violence courts with specialized prosecutors in three different states found augmented probation conditions as compared to jurisdictions without domestic violence specialization. Augmented conditions included drug and alcohol abstinence and testing, batterer intervention programs that lasted longer and were more expensive, more no-contact protective orders, attendance at fatherhood programs or women"s groups for female offenders, more mental health evaluations, mandatory employment and restrictions on weapons. [103]

Studies of four jurisdictions with specialized prosecution programs in as many states document that incarceration rates ranged from 20 to 76 percent. Most offenders were placed on probation and had to agree to no victim contact and attendance in a batterer treatment program. [196]

In at least one state, imprisonment of domestic violence felons has mushroomed over the last decade and a half. The number of domestic violence offenders sent to Ohio prisons increased nine-fold between 1991 and 2005. [225]

> **Performance Measure:** By statute, Calif. Penal Code §1203.097, California batterers must be sentenced to three years probation; criminal protective orders must be incorporated to protect victims from further violence, threats, stalking, sexual abuse and harassment; the defendant must complete a batterer program of no less than one year, make a minimum $200 payment, perform a specified amount of community service, attend a substance abuse treatment program as needed, pay restitution and, in lieu of a fine, pay up to $5,000 to a battered women"s shelter.

6.14 Does prosecuting domestic violence offenders deter reabuse?

The research is fairly consistent. Simply prosecuting offenders without regard to the specific risk they pose, unlike arresting domestic violence defendants, does not deter further criminal abuse. [11, 39, 55, 68, 96] The minority of abusers arrested who are low risk are unlikely to reabuse in the short run, whether prosecuted or not. Alternatively, without the imposition of significant sanctions including incarceration, the majority of arrested abusers who are high risk will reabuse regardless of prosecution — many while the case against them is pending.

A study of a large number of arrests in three states (Connecticut, Idaho and Virginia) found that those who were prosecuted and convicted for domestic violence were *more* likely to be rearrested than offenders who were not convicted. However, in this study, those prosecuted and convicted were significantly more likely to be higher risk offenders as measured by prior criminal history. [117]

A number of studies have found that prosecution can reduce subsequent arrests and violence. [66, 91, 130, 211, 225, 226] The key to reducing reabuse may depend not on whether the case is prosecuted but on the dispositions imposed. For example, a Toledo, Ohio, misdemeanor court study found that conviction was significantly associated with reduced rearrests for domestic violence one year following court disposition, even when controlling for batterers" prior history of domestic violence arrests, age, gender, education, employment, and marital status. However, the details of the specific disposition mattered. The more intrusive sentences — including jail, work release, electronic monitoring and/or probation — significantly reduced rearrest for domestic violence as compared to the less intrusive sentences of fines or suspended sentences without probation. The difference was statistically significant: Rearrests were 23.3 percent for defendants with more intrusive dispositions and 66 percent for those with less intrusive dispositions. [216]

Another study of 683 defendants in Hamilton County (Cincinnati), Ohio, who were arrested for misdemeanor domestic violence also confirmed that sentence severity was significantly associated with reduced recidivism, especially for unmarried defendants, although in this study the actual sentence length (number of days in jail) was not found to be significant. [206] Similar research looking at the cumulative effects of arrest followed by prosecution and court dispositions (including those receiving batterer treatment) has found modest reductions in reabuse to be associated with greater post-arrest criminal justice involvement. [163, 204] Research of almost 2,000 domestic violence defendants in Alexandria, Va., found that, over a period of three and one-half years, repeat offenders were associating with those who had a prior criminal history and were *not* sentenced to incarceration for the study arrest during that period. This led researchers to recommend jail sentences for domestic violence defendants with any prior criminal history. [172]

The Ohio felony study, however, found mixed results between jail sentences and prison sentences. Although jail sentences were significantly related to lower odds of subsequent misdemeanor or felony intimate-partner assaults after two years, prison sentences were not significantly related. Although the likelihood of new charges was 9 percent less for those jailed (compared to those sentenced to probation), the likelihood was only 2 percent lower for those imprisoned, compared to those placed on probation. [225] This may simply reflect that the sample size in the study was too small to produce a statistically significant effect.

Implications for Prosecutors

Prosecution deters domestic violence if it adequately addresses abuser risk by imposing appropriately intrusive sentences, including supervised probation and incarceration. (Research basis: Although studies conflict with each other on the subject of abuse prosecution, those studies that researched prosecutions, and the resulting dispositions that addressed defendant risk, suggest that domestic violence prosecution can significantly deter reabuse.)

6.15 When does sentencing of domestic violence defendants not necessarily prevent reabuse?

Some dispositional studies suggest that domestic violence sentencing patterns differ from standard sentencing patterns. Surprisingly, domestic violence sentences often do not reflect defendants" prior criminal history, suggesting that prosecutors and/or judges may disregard prior records that are not domestic-violence-related. In the Ohio study, for example, researchers found no correlation between offenders" prior criminal histories and sentence severity. [11] Similarly, the Toledo, Ohio, study found that defendants with prior **felony** convictions were the *least* likely to be prosecuted and sentenced. [216] In contrast, in both Quincy, Mass., and Rhode Island, prior criminal history was significantly associated with severity of sentences. [23, 141] Sentences that do not reflect a defendant"s prior criminal history (and prior sentences) may suggest to the defendant that domestic violence offenses are not taken as seriously as other offenses.

Implications for Prosecutors

Domestic violence sentencing should reflect defendants" prior criminal histories as well as abuse histories, as both indicate risk of reabuse as well as general criminality. (Research basis: Disparate sentencing studies found inconsistent variables, including consideration of prior records.)

6.16 Are defendants who don't show up in court more at risk for reabusing than those who do?

A Chicago study found that no-show defendants prosecuted by a specialized prosecution team had a significantly greater number of post-arrests than those that showed up in court (0.78 vs. 0.46). [107] Although this has not been examined elsewhere, in a Berkeley arrest study, researchers similarly documented that having a pending warrant at the time of the domestic violence incident was a significant predictor of reabuse. [228] The Quincy, Mass., arrest study also found that suspects who fled the scene before the police arrived were significantly more likely to reabuse than those suspects arrested at the scene. [23]

Implications for Prosecutors

If defendants default in court before their sentencing, prosecutors should consider them at higher risk for reabusing. (Research basis: Although only one study looked at this issue directly, several others found the same association between defendant conduct — not showing up in court — and risk of reabusing their victim before being prosecuted for the original abuse.)

6.17 Can "first" offenders be safely diverted or discharged?

In many jurisdictions, a substantial proportion of domestic violence defendants are diverted or given dispositions without having guilty findings imposed. Often, these dispositions are given to "first" offenders. Notwithstanding this trend, a trio of studies has found that a minimum of a quarter of defendants so sentenced reabuse or violate the terms of their conditional release.

In the Quincy, Mass., arrest study, a quarter of the arrested defendants were continued, without a finding to be dismissed, if they remained arrest free for six months to one year. These dispositions were reserved for defendants with less serious prior criminal and domestic abuse histories. These defendants were half as likely to have had prior records for domestic violence or crimes against persons or to have been sentenced to probation previously. Unlike those sentenced to probation or jailed who began their criminal careers as teenagers, these defendants began theirs at an average age of 25. Nonetheless, a quarter of those continued without a finding were arrested or had new protective orders taken out against them within two years of their study arrest. Although this reabuse rate was still half that of defendants with more substantial prior criminal histories, it was substantially higher than prosecutors and judges had anticipated. [138] Similarly, a little more than a quarter of the abusers (27.5 percent) who were given a conditional discharge in Cook County violated the conditions. [107]

In Rhode Island, probationary sentences for domestic violence cases without underlying suspended sentences constitute an in-court diversion much like cases continued without a finding in Massachusetts. (A probationary sentence in Rhode Island does not constitute a conviction under state law and therefore does not count as a sentence enhancement to a former or subsequent conviction. In the study, those sentenced to probationary sentences were most likely to be "first" domestic violence offenders.) Although the average defendant given a suspended or split sentence had 1.1 and 1.9 prior domestic violence arrests, respectively, those sentenced to probation had 0.5 prior arrests. Nevertheless, the rearrest rate for domestic violence for probated defendants was 34.8 percent, compared to 43.6 percent for those given suspended sentences and 48.1 percent given split sentences. [141]

Implications for Prosecutors

Prosecutors must exercise caution in recommending case diversion or conditional discharges, even if abusers have minimal prior criminal histories. (Research basis: Limited site studies and broader research on offender risk previously cited.)

6.18 Do specialized prosecution units work?

There are a limited number of studies specifically devoted to specialized domestic violence prosecution programs. Because specific programs vary, including the resources expended, it is difficult to pinpoint what works and what does not. Also, in many instances, these programs coexist with specialized domestic violence courts and other programs that may affect outcomes independent of the prosecution programs. However, in general, the research suggests that these programs work well on a number of levels.

First, research indicates that victims generally report satisfaction with domestic violence prosecutions conducted by specialized prosecution teams. Increased satisfaction may translate into increased victim cooperation. For example, in Alexandria, Va., a study revealed that 90.2 percent of victims found prosecutors either very or somewhat helpful, a higher rating than that given to the police or a victim support service agency. The 90.2 percent satisfaction rate reported by Alexandria victims compares to only 67.3 percent for victims in Virginia Beach, a jurisdiction that did not have a specialized domestic violence response program by police, prosecutors or victim advocates. [172]

Similarly, in Cook County (Chicago), victims reported higher satisfaction with the specialized domestic violence prosecution unit than with the prosecutors who handled domestic violence outside the unit. The unit featured specially trained prosecutors and vertical prosecution, where one prosecutor handles the case from arraignment through final disposition. This unit also had its own victim advocates. The victims were also more likely to appear in court: 75 percent compared to 25 percent in domestic violence cases in jurisdictions with no specialized domestic violence unit. [107]

The latter finding was not unique. Although victims most commonly reported fear of retaliation as a barrier to their participation in prosecution, a three-state study found that the fear was reduced in sites with specialized domestic violence courts that also contained specialized prosecution programs and increased victim advocacy. [103] However, the same study found equal satisfaction with prosecutors in both demonstration sites and comparison sites that had no specialized court domestic violence programs. [103]

Second, specialized prosecution programs have significantly increased prosecution and conviction rates. The specialized prosecution unit in Cook County (Chicago) obtained a conviction rate of 71 percent compared to 50 percent obtained by the rest of the office for domestic violence cases. [107] In Milwaukee, the specialized domestic violence prosecution unit increased felony convictions five times over, once the unit was established. [104] Implementation of a specialized domestic violence prosecution unit in Champaign County, Ill., increased prosecutions by 18 percent, and overall domestic violence case dismissals decreased by 54 percent. Convictions increased by 22 percent. [109]

However, other studies suggest that specialized prosecution units must be adequately staffed to make a difference. The specialized prosecution unit in Mecklenburg County (Charlotte), N.C., obtained a much lower conviction rate (38 percent), akin to that obtained without specialized units. However, researchers noted that the unit was significantly understaffed, with only two prosecutors assigned to hundreds of cases annually. [68] Brooklyn"s specialized felony prosecution program within the Borough"s special felony domestic violence court increased convictions from 87 percent to 94 percent for felonies other than protection order violations and to 93 percent for violations. Although the rate was higher than before, the difference was not statistically significant. [164]

Third, specialized prosecution programs appear to be associated with more robust dispositions that also appear to be better monitored and enforced. A study of three domestic violence courts with specialized prosecutors in three different states found augmented probation conditions as compared to jurisdictions without domestic violence specialization. Augmented conditions included drug and alcohol abstinence and testing, batterer intervention programs that lasted longer and were more expensive, more no-contact protective orders, attendance at fatherhood programs or women"s groups for female offenders, more mental health evaluations, mandatory employment and restrictions on weapons. [103]

Implications for Prosecutors

If adequately funded, specialized domestic violence prosecution units, especially if associated with specialized domestic violence law enforcement units and courts, should increase domestic violence prosecutions and convictions, victim cooperation and satisfaction and, if dispositions are geared to defendant risk of reabuse, more victim safety. (Research basis: Multiple studies in disparate jurisdictions.)

6.19 What characterizes specialized prosecution units?

An analysis of dozens of responses of prosecutors" offices to domestic violence found that the following dimensions characterized their responses: (1) responsiveness to victims (treating them as if they were civil plaintiffs as opposed to treating them dispassionately as witnesses to a crime), (2) treatment of suspects, (3) expectations for victim participation in prosecution, (4) specialization, and (5) information utilization. [227] The specialized units in upstate New York, unlike in other prosecutors" offices, were more likely to track: (1) cases for specialized prosecution, (2) data to inform the pressing of charges for recidivists, (3) data to inform sentencing recommendations, and (4) routinely received police incident reports as well as police arrest reports. In addition, specialized domestic violence units were more likely to participate in task forces or coalitions involving other criminal justice and community agencies involved in responding to domestic violence. [227]

Performance Measure: Most large prosecutors" offices have special domestic violence units, allowing for innovations such as vertical prosecution for misdemeanors, improved case preparation, greater contact with victims, reduced caseloads and more malleable court scheduling. [160] One-third of prosecutors in small and medium-sized cities across upstate New York also had specialized domestic violence prosecution programs, half of which made victim advocates available to victims. [227] (Research basis: A 2000 mail survey of 200 of the largest jurisdictions in 45 counties of upstate New York.)

7. Judicial Responses

7.1 Does sentencing domestic violence offenders deter reabuse?

The research is fairly consistent. Simply prosecuting offenders without regard to the specific risk they pose, unlike arresting domestic violence defendants, does not deter further criminal abuse. [11, 39, 55, 68, 96] The minority of abusers arrested who are low risk are unlikely to reabuse in the short run, whether prosecuted or not. Alternatively, without the imposition of significant sanctions including incarceration, the majority of arrested abusers who are high risk will reabuse regardless of prosecution — many while the case against them is pending.

A study of a large number of arrests in three states (Connecticut, Idaho and Virginia) found that those who were prosecuted and convicted for domestic violence were *more* likely to be rearrested than offenders who were not convicted. However, in this study, those prosecuted and convicted were significantly more likely to be higher risk offenders as measured by prior criminal history. [117]

A number of studies have found that prosecution can reduce subsequent arrests and violence. [66, 91, 130, 211, 225, 226] The key to reducing reabuse may not depend on whether or not the case is prosecuted but on the dispositions imposed. For example, a Toledo, Ohio, misdemeanor court study found that conviction was significantly associated with reduced rearrests for domestic violence one year following court disposition, even when controlling for batterers" prior history of domestic violence arrests, age, gender, education, employment and marital status. However, the details of the specific disposition mattered. The more intrusive sentences — including jail, work release, electronic monitoring and/or probation — significantly reduced rearrest for domestic violence as compared to the less intrusive sentences of fines or suspended sentences without probation. The difference was statistically significant: rearrests were 23.3 percent for defendants with more intrusive dispositions and 66 percent for those with less intrusive dispositions. [216]

Another study of 683 defendants in Hamilton County (Cincinnati), Ohio, who were arrested for misdemeanor domestic violence also confirmed that sentence severity was significantly associated with reduced recidivism, especially for unmarried defendants, although in this study the actual sentence length (number of days in jail) was not found to be significant. [206] Similar research looking at the cumulative effects of arrest followed by prosecution and court dispositions (including those receiving batterer treatment) has found modest reductions in reabuse to be associated with greater post-arrest criminal justice involvement. [163, 204] Research of almost 2,000 domestic violence defendants in Alexandria, Va., found that, over a period of three and one-half years, repeat offenders were associating with those who had a prior criminal history and were *not* sentenced to incarceration for the study arrest during that period. This led researchers to recommend jail sentences for domestic violence defendants with any prior criminal history. [172]

The Ohio felony study, however, found mixed results between jail sentences and prison sentences. Although jail sentences were significantly related to lower odds of subsequent misdemeanor or felony intimate-partner assaults after two years, prison sentences were not significantly related. Although the likelihood of new charges was 9 percent less for those jailed (compared to those sentenced to probation), the likelihood was only 2 percent lower for those imprisoned, compared to those placed on probation. [225] This may simply reflect that the sample size in the study was too small to produce a statistically significant effect.

Implications for Judges

Simply imposing guilty findings may not reduce the risk of reabuse. Judges should consider more intrusive sentences, including incarceration, for repeat abusers and those with prior criminal histories. (Research basis: Although studies conflict with each other on the subject of abuse prosecution, several sentencing studies suggest that more intrusive sentences may significantly deter reabuse.)

7.2 Should judges follow victim preferences when determining sentences?

Although victim perceptions of the dangerousness of suspects have been found to be good predictors of subsequent revictimization [23, 112, 113], victim preferences on how the case should be disposed are not good predictors. The victims in the Quincy, Mass., study who wanted the charges dropped were as likely to be revictimized (51 percent vs. 48 percent after one year) as those who did not want the charges dropped. [23] Similarly, studies in New York found that victim cooperation with prosecutors did not predict recidivism. In other words, when judges imposed sentences to which victims objected, these victims were no more or less likely to be revictimized than victims who wanted their abusers to be prosecuted and sentenced. [145]

Implications for Judges

Although judges should be open to victims" views, they should explain to victims (and, as important, to defendants) that the court is obligated to determine sentences as it deems best, with or without victims" agreement. (Research basis: Only one study directly compared victim prosecution wishes and subsequent reabuse.)

7.3 What should the response be when the suspect is brought in on an arrest or court-default warrant?

A large percentage of alleged abusers leave the crime scene before law enforcement arrives. Where noted, absence rates range from 42 to 66 percent. [23, 50, 117, 227, 228] Pursuing them, including the issuance of warrants, is associated with reduced revictimization. [50] Pursuing absent suspects may be of particular utility because limited research finds that suspects who flee the scene before police arrive are significantly more likely to have prior criminal histories and higher reabuse rates than those arrested at the scene. [23] Similarly, another study also finds higher reabuse if the *victim* is gone when officers arrive. [228]

Similarly, decreasing defendant defaults may also be associated with reduced reabuse. A study of Cook County"s four misdemeanor domestic violence courts found that no-show defendants had a significantly greater number of new arrests than those who showed up in court (0.78 vs. 0.46). [107]

Implications for Judges

Judges should treat alleged abusers who are brought to court on warrants at least as seriously as those arrested at the scene, even if the defendant appeared "voluntarily" to clear up the warrant. (Research basis: Numerous studies confirm that a large proportion of abusers flee the scene; only one study has looked at differences in records of those who fled the scene and those who didn't.)

7.4 What are current abuser sentencing practices?

Just as prosecution rates vary widely, so does sentencing of domestic violence perpetrators, even though the vast majority of domestic violence defendants are prosecuted for misdemeanor assaults. Although the United States Civil Rights Commission and National Council of Juvenile and Family Court Judges have opposed the practice [57, 214], many jurisdictions routinely divert abuse cases. In the Brooklyn Misdemeanor Domestic Violence Court study of 9,157 cases in 2002, of those pleading or found guilty, 51 percent received a conditional discharge, 35 percent received jail, 7 percent received probation, 5 percent were ordered to complete community service and 1 percent were fined. [31]

In Chicago, a little less than a third were given conditional discharges, 24 percent received probation or court supervision, and 23 percent were sent to jail (including time served pending trial). [107] While in Massachusetts, where three-quarters of the suspects (74.1 percent) were charged with some form of assault and/or battery, a quarter of the defendants were diverted, a quarter placed on probation and 13.5 percent imprisoned. [23] In Ohio, of those found guilty, almost 70 percent were incarcerated, with the largest number incarcerated between 30 and 45 days, although 18.8 percent were incarcerated 150 to 180 days. [11] The number of domestic violence offenders sent to Ohio prisons increased nine-fold between 1991 and 2005. [225] In three different states with specialized prosecution programs, 52 percent to 76 percent of convicted abusers were incarcerated. [196]

If placed on probation, supervision ranges from unsupervised to intensive, with a variety of special conditions. Most defendants in the specialized prosecution courts along with jail were placed on probation with a condition of no victim contact, undergoing batterer treatment, drug and alcohol abstinence and testing, attendance at fatherhood programs or women"s groups for female offenders, mental health evaluations, mandatory employment and restrictions on weapons. [103] A study of over a thousand domestic violence arrests across three states, Connecticut, Idaho and Virginia, found that, of those convicted, a little less than half (46.7 percent) were ordered into either anger management or batterer programs. [117]

By statute, Cal. Penal Code §1203.097, California batterers must be sentenced to three years probation; criminal protective orders must be incorporated to protect victims from further violence, threats, stalking, sexual abuse and harassment; the defendant must complete a batterer program of no less than a year, make a minimum $200 payment, and perform a specified amount of community service as well as attending substance abuse treatment as needed, pay restitution and, in lieu of a fine, pay up to $5,000 to a battered women"s shelter. However, a 2005 study revealed widespread variance with the law in practice by allowing defendants to plead guilty to nondomestic violence crimes such as assault or trespass. [149]

7.5 What accounts for dispositions?

The research suggests that domestic violence dispositions do not always follow standard sentencing patterns, often not reflecting defendants" prior criminal histories, suggesting that prosecutors and judges disregard prior records that are not related to domestic violence charges. In a large Ohio court study, for example, researchers found no correlation between offenders" prior criminal histories and sentence severity. [11] Similarly and surprisingly, the Toledo, Ohio, study found defendants with prior **felony** convictions were the least likely to be prosecuted and sentenced. [216] In contrast, in both Quincy, Mass., and Rhode Island, prior criminal history was significantly associated with the severity of sentences. [23, 141]

Victim preference was not found to be a significant factor in sentencing in Quincy, Mass., Everett, Wash., Klamath Falls, Ore., Omaha, Neb., San Diego, Calif., or Ohio. [11, 23, 196] In these jurisdictions, factors associated with more severe sentences varied considerably and included whether there was strangulation, the gender of the defendant, whether the defendant and victim were living together, the size of the prosecutor"s caseload, and so on. No consistent patterns were noted from study to study.

Implications for Judges

Sentences should reflect defendants" prior criminal histories as well as abuse histories, as both indicate risk of reabuse as well as general criminality. It is a mistake for judges to consider abusers with prior criminal histories as "first offenders" simply because they have no prior record specifically for domestic violence. (Research basis: Disparate sentencing studies find inconsistent variables including consideration of prior records.)

7.6 Are defendants who don't show up in court more at risk for reabuse than those who do?

The Chicago study found that no-show defendants prosecuted by a specialized prosecution team had a significantly greater number of post-arrests than those that showed (0.78 vs. 0.46). [107] While this has not been examined elsewhere, in a Berkeley arrest study, researchers similarly documented that having a pending warrant at the time of the domestic violence incident was a significant predictor of reabuse. [228] The Quincy, Mass., arrest study also found that suspects who flee the scene before police arrived were significantly more likely to reabuse than those arrested at the scene. [23]

Implications for Judges

If defendants default in court prior to sentencing, judges should consider them higher risk for reabuse for purposes of bail, fashioning civil orders and sentencing. (Research basis: Although only one study looked at this issue directly, several others found the same association between defendant conduct and reabuse pre-prosecution.)

7.7 Can "first" offenders be safely diverted or discharged?

The few studies that have examined reabuse among diverted or discharged abusers have consistently found that a steady minority continued to reabuse, notwithstanding no or minimal prior records. In the Quincy arrest study, for example, a quarter of the arrested defendants were continued, without a finding to be dismissed, if they remained arrest free for six months to a year, a disposition reserved for first or lesser defendants. A quarter were arrested or had new protective orders taken out against them within two years of their study arrest. Although this reabuse rate was still half that of defendants with more substantial prior criminal histories, it was substantially higher than prosecutors and judges had anticipated. [138] Similarly, a little over a quarter of the abusers (27.5 percent) given a conditional discharge in Cook County violated the conditional discharge. [107] While those placed on probation in Rhode Island with guilty findings was higher than those placed on probation without guilty findings, the rearrest rate for domestic violence over one year was still 35 percent. [141]

Implications for Judges

Judges cannot assume that defendants with no or limited prior records for domestic violence can be diverted pre-adjudication or given conditional discharges without consistently compromising safety for at least a quarter of their victims. (Research basis: Limited site studies as well as broader research on offender risk previously cited.)

7.8 Who obtains civil protective orders?

The research suggests that abusers brought to court for civil protective orders differ little from their peers arrested by police for domestic abuse. Studies have found that they have equivalent criminal histories, ranging from 65 percent in a study of respondents in Denver, Delaware and the District of Columbia [133] to a little more than 70 percent in a Texas study [26] and 80 percent in a Massachusetts study. [134] Another Massachusetts study of protective order violators found that 80 percent had a prior record, including 69 percent who were charged for a prior nondomestic but violent offense. [2]

One of the reasons for the substantial overlap between abusers brought to court for civil orders and those arrested for abuse by police is that many petitioners come to civil court as a result of police encouragement following an abuse incident involving police. In a multicourt study, 43 percent of victims who obtained civil protective orders said they either learned of the orders or were encouraged to apply for them by police responding to a domestic violence incident. [182]

Implications for Judges

Victims seeking civil remedies for abuse are at the same level of risk for reabuse as victims of abusers arrested for abusing them. (Research basis: Extensive research of civil petitioners that was conducted in disparate jurisdictions.)

7.9 When and why do victims ask for orders?

Researchers agree that most victims do not request civil orders after the first abuse incident or assault. According to the NVAW survey, only 16.4 percent of rape victims, 17.1 percent of assault victims, and 36.6 percent of stalking victims petitioned for protective orders following an abuse incident. [209] A survey of victims in battered women"s shelters found that only 40 percent had obtained protective orders before fleeing their homes and entering the shelter. [178] Finally, several studies based on samples of women who reported abuse to police found that only 12 to 22 percent had secured protective orders. [120, 220]

Often, victims petition courts for orders after failing to stem the abuse through other means. In a multicourt study involving both an inner city minority jurisdiction and a suburban nonminority city south of Boston, female victims had tried to protect themselves in a variety of other ways before petitioning court for an order. Perhaps most significantly, 68 percent had left their abuser at least once, and 15 percent had kicked their abuser out of the home at least once before petitioning the courts for orders. In addition, 78 percent had called police at least once before, 30 percent had obtained counseling, and 25 percent had called a hotline or had gone to a shelter. [182] In a Colorado study, half of the petitioners had left their abusers at the time of the incident that provoked the protective order petition. [105] Studies have found that between 27 and 50 percent of victims are living with their abuser at the time of the incident that prompted the order request [106, 133, 182], whereas between 37 and 46 percent file for orders after they have left. [74, 75]

As a result, most victims who petition courts for protection orders have suffered several years of abuse with the same abuser before coming to court for the first time. In a multistate (and District of Columbia) study, researchers found that only 10 percent sought protection orders after a week of abuse, 15 percent experienced abuse for one to two years, and nearly 25 percent had endured abuse for more than five years. [133] In a Colorado study, the average female petitioner suffered 12.74 abusive behaviors in the year before requesting their orders (e.g., being threatened to being raped). About 20 percent reported that their prior abuse included the more serious behaviors, including strangling, forced sex and beating. The duration ranged from once to 31 years, with a median of 2.4 years. [105]

The specific incident that prompted victims to petition for protective orders generally involved physical abuse. In the multistate (and District of Columbia) study, more than a third had been threatened or injured with a weapon (36.8 percent), more than half (54.4 percent) had experienced severe physical abuse, 83.9 percent experienced mild physical abuse, and almost all (98.9 percent) had been intimidated through threats, stalking and harassment. [133] In Quincy, Mass., almost two-thirds (64.4 percent) of the victims were physically assaulted, and another third had been threatened with death or harm to them, their children or a relative. [134] Similarly, in a Colorado study, 56 percent of the female petitioners had sustained physical injuries during the incident that led to the protective order requests. [105] In the two courts studied in Massachusetts (one located in a minority neighborhood of Boston, the other a south shore mid-sized city), 92 percent of the petitions filed by female victims described incidents that constituted criminal acts, and 70 percent of them constituted assault and battery. Breaking down the affidavits further, the researcher found that 48 percent described separation violence; 22 percent described punishment, coercion and retaliation concerning children; and 12 percent described retaliation for calling police. A total of 65 percent of the female petitioners told the researcher that the abuser had threatened them with death, 35 percent had visited hospitals as a result of prior violence in the past, 30 percent suffered sexual abuse and, of those who were mothers, 51 percent reported threats to take children from them or report them as unfit to child protective services. [182]

On the other hand, the incident that prompts victims to seek orders may not be the most serious incident they experienced at the hand of their abusers. Research has found that the seriousness of the incident itself is not predictive of a future risk of reabuse. [23, 39, 134, 141, 145, 172]

Implications for Judges

Although petitions focus on the most recent, discrete incident, the incident rarely reveals fully the nature of the abuse suffered by the petitioner or the risk for future abuse. Post-separation abuse frequently involves stalking behavior, a risk factor for further abuse, and even lethality. To obtain more information, judges need to further question victims and review respondents" prior criminal and civil history. (Research basis: Extensive studies of petitioners in disparate jurisdictions as well as many abuser studies.)

7.10 How many abusers violate court protective orders?

Research varies, but violation rates have been found to range from 23 percent over two years [26], 35 percent within six months [133], to 60 percent within twelve months [105], and in between at 48.8 percent within two years. [134] A Rhode Island study found consistent violation of criminal no-contact orders imposed after domestic violence arrests, resulting in subsequent concurrent sentences for both the initial domestic violence offense and the no-contact violation. Furthermore, the study also found that the majority (51 percent) of abusers sentenced concurrently for abuse-related offenses and no-contact violations reabused their victims. The rearrest rate for new abuse for abusers specifically convicted of civil protection order violations was 44 percent, and for criminal no-contact orders it was 48 percent, higher than all other domestic violence offenses, which ranged from 25 to 39 percent. [141]

The actual rates of violation of protective orders are higher if reabuse is measured by new domestic violence arrests or victim self-reports. In addition, order violation rates may not accurately reflect reabuse over a specific period of time because many victims do not retain or decide to drop orders. Although "permanent orders" in Massachusetts are for one year, almost half of the female victims subsequently returned to court to drop their orders before the year ended. [134] A review of disparate jurisdictions revealed that retention rates varied from 16 percent in Omaha, Neb., in 2003 [135] to 69 percent in the District of Columbia in 2000 [200] and 80 percent in East Norfolk, Mass., in 1995. [134]

Implications for Judges

As with the arrest of abusers, the issuance of protective orders alone does not assure victims" safety. Judges should advise victims of their protective order limitations. (Research basis: Multiple studies in disparate jurisdictions.)

7.11 Do protective orders work?

The research has not been able to answer this question definitively, mainly because it is not ethically permissible to randomly grant or deny protective orders to compare results. Furthermore, these orders may "work" at different levels.

First, in terms of their effectiveness in deterring repeat abuse, before and after studies suggest that protective orders may deter certain abusers. In Travis County, Texas, over a period of two years before and after order issuance, physical abuse dropped from 68 percent to 23 percent after the orders were obtained, if victims maintained the order. If the abusers were also arrested at the time of the order issuance, the physical abuse diminished further; if they had children, it diminished less. [26] These studies cannot reveal whether or not the abuse would have naturally declined overtime without the orders because, for example, the victims are more likely to have left their abusers when they obtained the orders.

Several Seattle studies compared women who obtained orders to women who were abused (as indicated by a police incident report) but did not obtain orders. They found that women with permanent orders were less likely to be physically abused than women without them. However, women who had temporary orders that lasted only two weeks were more likely to be psychologically abused than women who did not obtain any orders. The women who did not obtain orders appeared at higher risk for abuse, involvement with alcohol and drugs, more likely to have been assaulted and injured as a result of the study incident, and less likely to have been married to their abuser. The study did not look at violations of protective orders that did not involve physical assaults. [120] The second Seattle study found that the orders were more effective nine months after they were obtained than during the first five-month period, significantly reducing the likelihood of contact, threats with weapons, injuries and the need for medical care. [121]

Finally, several other studies that compared women who maintained orders and those who dropped them, or did not return for permanent orders, found that order retention made no difference in reabuse rates. [105, 134] A Rhode Island study involving criminal no-contact orders, issued automatically during a domestic violence arrest, also found that whether victims allowed the orders to be continued for the length of the criminal case and probationary sentences that followed (usually one year) or not, the reabuse rates did not vary. [141]

At least one study suggests that the specific stipulations of the protective orders may make a difference. Specifically, victims are more likely to be reabused if their orders bar abusive contact but not all contact. Compared to women whose orders barred all contact, those that barred only abusive contact were significantly more likely to suffer psychological violence, physical violence, sexual coercion and injuries within one year. [150]

Nonetheless, the research consistently finds that victims largely express satisfaction with civil orders, even if they are violated by their abusers. [134] In the multisite study in Massachusetts, 86 percent of the women who obtained a permanent order said that the order either stopped or reduced the abuse, notwithstanding the fact that 59 percent called police to report an order violation. Upon further questioning, the women expressed the feeling that the order demonstrated to the abuser that the "law was on her side." [182] In a multistate study, victims who obtained orders reported that the orders improved their overall well-being, especially if the abuser had a prior criminal history and were more likely to reabuse. [133] It may be that, even though orders do not stop abuse, they reduce the severity of the reabuse. Alternatively, although they may not affect the extent of reabuse, protective orders make victims feel vindicated and empowered.

Although not studied directly, it appears to be significantly easier for law enforcement to monitor and enforce protective and no-contact orders than to monitor and interrupt abuse in general. This may explain why abusers are significantly more likely to be arrested for protective order violations than other common domestic violence offenses. The rearrest rate for abusers in Rhode Island initially arrested for violation of protection or no-contact orders was 45.6 percent over one year, compared to 37.6 percent for domestic assaults, disorderly conduct or vandalism. [141] Of course, it may also be the case that abusers with orders are generally at higher risk for reabusing than abusers without orders.

Implications for Judges

Victims should be encouraged to take out protective orders and retain them but should also be advised that the orders do not deter all abusers and may be more effective when accompanied by criminal prosecution of the abuser. (Research basis: Numerous studies indicating consistent victim satisfaction with orders, complemented by studies that have consistently found that orders do not appear to significantly increase the risk of reabuse and may deter some abusers.)

7.12 Does judicial demeanor make a difference?

Although few studies have looked at judicial conduct specifically, a multisite study in Massachusetts found that judges issuing orders fell into three categories: (1) those with "good-natured demeanors," who were supportive and informative with victims and firm with abusers; (2) those with "bureaucratic demeanors," who were firm and formal with all parties; and (3) those with "condescending, harsh and demeaning demeanors" but who were often good-natured with abusers. The research found that victims felt more empowered, listened to, and were more likely to retain orders issued by the first category of judges rather than the two other groups. The first group was also more likely to cooperate with prosecutors on concurrent criminal charges against the abusers. Most of the judges were found to be in the first group. [182]

Another study compared two Massachusetts courts within 10 miles of each other. One court was characterized as "user friendly" for victims, with a special office for victims to complete forms as well as special court sessions so petitioners did not have to wait to see judges. The other court was more bureaucratic, with no special offices or sessions for victims. Victims in the first court had an 80 percent retention rate (i.e., they returned to obtain permanent orders after the temporary orders expired), whereas those in the other court had a 20 percent return rate. [101] Similarly and perhaps for the same reason, specialized domestic violence courts have also been found to increase victim order retention rates. A study of a District of Columbia domestic violence court found that it increased retention from 40 to 55 percent after imposition of the specialized domestic violence sessions. [200]

In a related study of upstate New York courts, a study across multiple jurisdictions found that the demeanor of the judge also reverberated across the criminal justice system. It found that, even compared to a "rights-oriented" judge who held police and prosecutors to a high evidentiary standard (which they often met), a judge who strongly believed that domestic violence cases did not belong in court stifled and discouraged both domestic violence arrests in the community and prosecutions in court. [227]

Implications for Judges

Judges should strive to create user-friendly, safe court environments for petitioners, be sympathetic to the parties before them, but firm with respondents once abuse has been determined. Thus, victim concerns are validated, and respondents" abusive behaviors are clearly condemned. (Research basis: Limited studies confined to three different court jurisdictions in Massachusetts.)

7.13 Do specialized domestic violence courts work?

Although relatively new, some research shows that specialized domestic violence courts are associated with decreased reoffending and reabuse. The reduction may be due to reforms of court processes or a corresponding specialization of domestic violence prosecution and/or probation supervision, or all three. A study of Milwaukee"s federally funded domestic violence court found that the number of arrests were halved for domestic violence defendants sentenced to probation, compared to those sentenced to probation before court reform. The rearrest rate dropped from 8 percent to 4.2 percent. The average number of new arrests also dropped significantly. Researchers posited that one of the prime explanations for the drop was a corresponding rise in the use of incarceration as a sentence. As a result of tight judicial monitoring and enforcement of release conditions, the post-reform probationers spent 13,902 days confined, compared to the 1,059 days probationers spent jailed in the days before court reform. In other words, those sentenced by the special domestic violence court had less time on the streets to reabuse and reoffend. [104]

Studies also found reduced reabuse rates at one other federally funded domestic violence court, in Dorchester, Mass., over a period of 11 months, but not in a third model domestic violence court examined in Michigan. In all three sites, researchers found that the courts were most effective with 18- to 29-year-old defendants, and offenders with seven or more prior arrests whose victims had moderate to high support, did not have children with their abusers, and whose relationship with them was less than three years. Although reabuse declined in two of the courts, overall new arrests for any offense were not statistically different, although they were in the expected direction: 22 percent for the domestic violence courts, and 28 percent for the nondomestic violence courts. [103]

Three other studies of specialized domestic violence courts have found small but significant reductions in reoffending [79, 91], including a study of the San Diego superior court, in which rearrests dropped from 21 to 14 percent in one year. [180] An evaluation of Cook County's four domestic violence courts, on the other hand, found no differences in rearrest rates over six months. [107]

Apart from reduced reabuse rates, domestic violence courts are associated with increased convictions and decreased dismissals. [40, 104, 115, 164] In Cook County, the four misdemeanor domestic violence courts significantly increased the likelihood of victims appearing in court when compared with their appearance in general courts (73 vs. 40 percent). This, in turn, correlated with increased conviction rates of 73 percent in domestic violence courts compared to 22.9 percent in general courts. [107]

Although domestic violence victims generally rate their court experiences highly, they rate domestic violence courts even more highly. [52, 91, 124] One study found that if victims were aware that there was a domestic violence court, three-quarters of the victims were more likely to report future violence. [196] One of the reasons that victims may prefer domestic violence courts may be the court contacts providing increased victim services and referrals to victim advocates, documented in several of the studies. [103, 115, 164] This may be why the District of Columbia domestic violence court was able to report an increased rate of civil protective order retention from 40 to 55 percent. [200] Domestic violence courts are also associated with more efficient processing of cases. The study of Manhattan's domestic violence misdemeanor court experienced faster case processing as well as improved identification of domestic violence cases. [179]

The research also finds that domestic violence courts increase offender compliance by imposing court-ordered conditions and by increasing in the penalties for noncompliance. [104, 164] The study of Manhattan's domestic violence misdemeanor court documented enhanced monitoring of offenders after their convictions. [179] Defendants in Milwaukee were required to attend post-disposition court reviews 60 to 90 days after disposition. In 2002, the court conducted 1,347 such reviews, and probation revocations increased dramatically. [104]

Implications for Judges

Specialized domestic violence courts are associated with beneficial reforms in several areas, including victim safety and satisfaction, offender accountability, and more efficient case-flow processing. (Research basis: The research is based mainly on disparate process evaluations of specialized domestic violence courts. The research does not suggest, however, that judges presiding over general trial courts cannot adopt similar practices and thereby achieve the same results in each case.)

7.14 What makes specialized domestic violence courts different?

A 2004 study found 160 jurisdictions across the country with specialized domestic violence courts. The majority of these courts had the following traits in common: (1) effective management of domestic violence cases, coordinating all of the cases involving the relevant parties and integrating requisite information for the court; (2) specialized intake and court staffing for domestic violence cases; (3) improved victim access, expedited hearings, and assistance for victims by court staff, often assisted by related specialized, vertical domestic violence prosecution units; (4) court processes to ensure victims" safety (e.g., court metal detectors, separate waiting rooms, specialized orders and victim referrals; (5) increased court monitoring and enforcement of batterer compliance with court orders, often exercised by specialized probation supervision units; (6) consideration of any children involved in the domestic violence; and (7) enhanced domestic violence training for judges. [132]

Pretrial Monitoring of Defendants

In the specialized domestic violence court in San Diego, Calif., a bail amount of $10,000 surety or $1,000 cash is standard for each misdemeanor domestic violence charge. In Everett, Wash., $10,000 is the typical bail, without a cash alternative. Increases in the holding of defendants pretrial has been shown to increase plea bargains at arraignment. In San Diego, 46 percent of defendants were found to plead at arraignment. [196] After establishment of a specialized domestic violence court in Milwaukee, 20 percent plead guilty before they were assigned a trial date. [103, 104] Increased restrictions on defendant-victim contact have also been found to increase the likelihood of conviction. [103, 104]

Decreasing defendant defaults may also be associated with reduced reabuse. A study of Cook County"s four misdemeanor domestic violence courts found that no-show defendants had a significantly greater number of new arrests than those who showed in court (0.78 vs. 0.46). [107] This is consistent with research that found that defendants who flee the abuse incident before police arrive are twice as likely to reabuse than those who remain at the scene of the incident. [23]

As a result of enhanced pretrial processing after the establishment of the specialized court, convictions through guilty pleas increased and trials decreased in the Brooklyn (Kings County), N.Y., felony domestic violence court, while the conviction rate remained the same. [164]

Implications for Judges. Judicial attention before trial to address the risk to victims posed by alleged abusers will result in quicker case resolution and decrease reabuse by defendants who fail to show for trial. (Research basis: Multiple studies from multiple jurisdictions.)

Enhanced Court Dispositions

Court dispositions in specialized domestic violence courts tend to be more substantial than elsewhere and more rigorously enforced. In Everett, Wash., and Klamath Falls, Ore., defendants were more likely to be ordered to attend batterer intervention programs and drug counseling and to be ordered to abstain from drugs and submit to testing. Furthermore, the batterer intervention programs increased in length and cost. At these and other sites with specialized court programs, defendants were more likely to be ordered to have no contact with their victims. [196] In terms of enforcement, in Milwaukee, a study revealed that after implementation of the specialized domestic violence court system, there was a dramatic increase in probation revocations (27 percent compared to the previous 2 percent). Most revocations (70 percent) were for technical violations such as failure to attend batterer intervention programs. [104]

In Massachusetts and Cook County, Ill., specialized domestic violence courts reduced deferred prosecutions and increased the percentage of defendants who were sentenced to jail time. Court conviction rates in the latter rose from 50 percent to 71.4 percent; the likelihood of jail increased significantly from 6.7 percent to 31.3 percent. [107]

Implications for Judges. Judges presiding over specialized domestic violence courts appear more likely to impose more intrusive sanctions against convicted abusers. (Research basis: Disparate studies demonstrate a correlation, although specialized domestic violence courts may offer judges enhanced dispositional options, including specialized probationary supervision programs for abusers. These specialized courts may also have judges who are better informed about domestic violence than other judges.)

7.15 Do enhanced domestic violence dispositions require enhanced postdisposition court time and resources?

Studies have found that enhanced sentencing of abusers involving probation with relevant conditions (e.g., batterer programs, abstinence or no-contact orders) requires enhanced monitoring because many abuser probationers typically fail to comply.

Studies have documented that noncompliance rates prompting formal revocations of probation ranged from 12 percent in the Dorchester, Mass., courts to 27 percent in Milwaukee misdemeanor domestic violence courts. [103] In Cook County"s four misdemeanor domestic violence courts, the revocation rate was 27.5 percent. [107] Higher rates were found in a series of other studies of domestic violence supervision programs across Illinois: 38.5 percent in Sangamond (Springfield) County, 33 percent in Peoria, and 22.8 percent in Tazewell County. The revocation rate was more than 50 percent in Quincy, Mass. [108, 109, 138] In Brooklyn"s felony domestic violence court, the rate was 33 percent. [164]

Revocation rates may reflect probation resources and policies as much as they reflect probationers" conduct. For example, an evaluation of Rhode Island"s specialized domestic violence probation supervision unit found that the unit"s probation revocation rate was 44 percent, whereas the rate for comparable abuse probationers supervised in larger mixed caseloads during the same period was only 24.7 percent. Almost all of the violations were for noncompliance with the state"s mandated batterer intervention program. [141]

Implications for Judges

Enhanced dispositions increase the likelihood of technical violations, which require additional judicial time if defendants are to be held accountable. (Research basis: Multiple studies in disparate jurisdictions.)

7.16 Does the type of postdispositional monitoring matter?

Studies are mixed concerning the impact of postdisposition judicial monitoring, which probably should not be surprising because the quality of judicial monitoring is undoubtedly mixed as well. For example, a quasi-experimental study involving the Bronx domestic violence court found that judicial monitoring did not reduce recidivism, although there was a modest but transitory one-year reduction in domestic violence arrests. However, the same study found the quality of the monitoring program to be problematic. [185] A study of the San Diego court system attributed a decrease in rearrests, from 21 to 14 percent in one year, to judicial monitoring. [180] Other studies also suggest that a longer period of court control is associated with reduced reabuse. [42] Increased pretrial court appearances have also been associated with decreased reabuse. [179]

Studies have also found that probation supervision increases the number of offenders who complete batterer intervention programs. A multiyear study across Massachusetts found that the batterer program completion rate was 62 percent for those offenders whose cases were supervised but was only 30 percent for those whose cases were unsupervised. [18]

Implications for Judges

Postdispositional patterns of compliance and enforcement should be reviewed periodically to ensure that the crucial role of judges" postdisposition is being fulfilled. (Research basis: Several studies in disparate jurisdictions are suggestive but, given the variety of court contexts, no specific model of a postdispositional monitoring program has emerged, or is likely to emerge, as better than any other.)

7.17 Does probation supervision of abusers reduce likelihood of reabuse?

A few studies of probation supervision of abusers have been conducted. A quasi-experimental study across the state of Rhode Island found that those abusers who were supervised in a specialized domestic violence probation program — featuring victim contact, slightly more intensive supervision of abusers (twice a month), intensive monitoring of mandated batterer intervention programs, and probation officers who volunteered to supervise these caseloads — were significantly less likely to commit new offenses and abuse within one year, but this applied only to those probationers who had not been on probation previously. [137, 141]

Although specialized domestic violence courts often involve specialized probation supervision programs, probation"s contribution to these courts" successes (and failures) has not been studied separately. The cumulative effect of probation monitoring and counseling completion has been found to significantly lower recidivism. [163] Another researcher has found that enhanced domestic-violence supervision programs have reduced reoffending compared to nonenhanced supervision. [108]

Implications for Judges

Specialized supervision of abusers may help reduce reabuse. (Research basis: Tentative findings based on only limited studies.)

8. Intervention Programs

8.1 Do batterer intervention programs prevent reabuse?

Commonly, whether diverted, probated or jailed, many domestic violence offenders are required to attend batterer intervention programs. These programs have increased dramatically over the past several decades. [110]

During this time, there have been more than 35 evaluations of batterer intervention programs, but they have yielded inconsistent results. Two meta-analyses of the more rigorous studies find the programs have, at best, a "modest" treatment effect, producing a minimal reduction in re-arrests for domestic violence. [8, 62] In one of the meta-analyses, the treatment effect translated to a 5-percent improvement rate in cessation of reassaults due to the treatment. [8] In the other, it ranged from none to 0.26, roughly representing a reduction in recidivism from 13 to 20 percent. [62]

On the other hand, a few studies have found that batterer intervention programs make abusers more likely to reabuse [90, 102] or have found no reduction in abuse at all. [36, 42, 61] The multistate study of four batterer programs concludes that approximately a quarter of batterers appear unresponsive and resistant to batterer intervention. In this long-term study, based on victim and/or abuser interviews and/or police arrests, approximately half of the batterers reassaulted their initial or new partners sometime during the study's 30-month follow-up. Most of the reassaults occurred within the first six months of program intake. Nearly a quarter of the batterers repeatedly assaulted their partners during the follow-up and accounted for nearly all of the severe assaults and injuries. [84, 85, 88]

Implications for Prosecutors and Judges

Batterer programs, in and of themselves, are not likely to protect most victims or new intimate partners of referred abusers from further harm from higher risk abusers. Consequently, if mandated or utilized, batterer intervention programs should be supplemented by other measures to assure victim safety from these abusers. (Research basis: Multiple single studies as well as two meta-analyses of studies from disparate jurisdictions in different contexts across the country.)

8.2 Does the type or length of batterer intervention program make a difference?

Several studies have found that the type of batterer intervention program, whether feminist, psycho-educational, or cognitive-behavioral, does not affect reabuse. [8, 51, 88] One study also found that a "culturally focused" program specifically designed for black male abusers did no better than the program offered to all abusers. In fact, those assigned to a conventional, racially mixed group were half as likely to be arrested for reassaults compared to those assigned to a black culturally focused counseling group or a conventional group of all blacks. [87]

However, a rigorous study based in New York City found the length of the program (26 weeks compared to 8 weeks) may make a difference, with the longer program proving more effective at deterring reabuse. The researchers suggest that the longer program's increased effectiveness was due to its longer suppression effect while abusers were mandated to attend, whether or not they actually attended. [42] On the other hand, a multistate study of four programs ranging in length from 3 to 9 months found no difference in subsequent reabuse. [84, 85, 88]

Implications for Prosecutors and Judges

As long as the batterer intervention program is focused on preventing reabuse, the type of program makes no difference. However, longer batterer programs may be better than shorter programs. (Research basis: Although only one study speaks to the suppression effects of batterer programs, the finding that batterer programs provide little treatment effect suggests that programs" effectiveness may result from their suppression effect and/or the context in which they operate, including probation supervision or periodic court compliance hearings. These findings argue for longer programs.)

> **Performance Measure:** By statute, batterer intervention programs mandated for convicted abusers in California Penal Code §1203.097(A)(6) must be conducted for two hours each week and for a minimum of 52 consecutive weeks.

8.3 Do couples counseling or anger management treatment programs prevent reabuse?

There has been little recent research on the application of couples counseling involving batterers and their victims [201] as most batterer treatment standards prohibit couples counseling. [7] While an early study in 1985 found it ineffective, with half of the couples reporting new violence within six weeks of couples counseling [148], other studies found lower reabuse rates. [47] A small study suggests that couples counseling *after* separate counseling for batterers and victims may be safe and beneficial for couples who want to remain together. [129]

Although anger management is often part of batterer intervention programs based on cognitive psychology, most state batterer treatment standards prohibit generic anger management programs or couples counseling as alternative forms of treatment on their own. [7]

In one of the largest studies to date, the Office of the Commissioner of Probation in Massachusetts studied a sample of 945 defendants arraigned for violating a protective order. As part of their subsequent disposition, they were ordered into a certified batterer intervention program, anger management program, and/or a mental health treatment or substance abuse treatment program; 13 percent were sent to multiple programs. The study found that those referred to 12- to 20-week anger management programs had a higher completion rate than those referred to the much longer 40-week batterer intervention programs. Higher completion rates notwithstanding, there was no difference in rearrest rates for those who completed anger management programs and those who failed to complete one. Furthermore, those who completed anger management programs recidivated at higher rates than those who completed batterer intervention programs, even though those referred to batterer intervention programs had significantly more criminal history, including more past order violations, more long-standing substance abuse histories, and less education than those referred to anger management programs. [18]

An earlier study of a program in Pittsburgh found that abusers who relied on anger management control techniques were more likely to reabuse their partners than those who relied on increased empathy, a redefinition of their manhood, and more cooperative decisionmaking as a means to ending their abuse. [80]

Implications for Prosecutors and Judges

There is no evidence that couples counseling or anger management programs effectively prevent court-referred batterers from reabusing or committing new offenses after treatment. (Research basis: The limited research conducted thus far has been, at best, inconclusive regarding the effectiveness of these programs. One large state study found that court-referred batterers are less apt to commit new offenses [including both domestic and nondomestic violence offenses] if they completed batterer programs rather than anger management programs. The difference, however, may be because the batterer programs were twice as long as the anger control programs.)

8.4 Does alcohol and drug treatment prevent reabuse?

The correlation between alcohol and drug treatment has been confirmed in numerous studies cited previously (also see question referring to perpetrators, "Are they likely to be drug and/or alcohol abusers?"). These studies find substance abuse treatment can be effective in reducing domestic violence. [203] In one such study, for example, researchers found that among 301 alcoholic male partner abusers, of whom 56 percent had physically abused their partners the year before treatment, partner violence significantly decreased for half a year after alcohol treatments but still was not as low as the nonalcoholic control group. Among those patients who remained sober, reabuse dropped to 15 percent, the same as the nonalcoholic control group and half that of treated alcoholics who failed to maintain sobriety. [169] As this study suggests, however, alcohol and drug treatment, in and of itself, may not be sufficient for all abusers. Supporting this is a Massachusetts treatment study of 945 defendants convicted of violating protective orders and subsequently ordered into a program. The study found that those who completed a variety of alcohol and drug treatment programs had higher rates of rearraignment over six years, for any crime or for violations of protective orders, than those who completed batterer intervention programs (57.9 vs. 47.7 percent for any crime, and 21.1 vs. 17.4 percent for violation of protective orders). Furthermore, there was no significant difference in rearraignment rates between those who completed the substance abuse treatment and those who did not. [18]

On the other hand, studies suggest alcohol and drug treatment may be a necessary component of successful intervention to prevent reabuse. The multistate study of four batterer programs found that, among those who completed the program, those who became intoxicated within a three-month period were three times more likely to reassault their partners than those who did not. [84, 85, 88]

Implications for Prosecutors and Judges

Incorporating alcohol and/or drug treatment as a standard component of batterer intervention programs adds to the likelihood of reductions in reabuse among batterers, many of whom abuse alcohol and drugs. Effective treatment should include abstinence testing to assure sobriety and no drug use. (Research basis: Extensive research in both clinical and court settings confirms the correlation between substance abuse and the increased likelihood of reabuse as well as the reduction in reabuse among offenders successfully treated for drug abuse.)

8.5 Are court-referred batterers likely to complete batterer programs?

Multiple studies of disparate programs around the country have found high noncompletion rates ranging from 25 percent to 89 percent, with most at around 50 percent. [36, 87, 183] Rates vary because different programs have different standards for monitoring attendance as well as different policies regarding re-enrollment, missed meetings, and so on. A study in California found that, of 10 counties examined, only one maintained a database to track offender participation in the mandated batterer intervention program; it reported that 89 percent did not complete the program. [149]

Not surprisingly, adding on additional treatment programs increases noncompletion. For example, although 42 percent of the referred batterers in the Bronx court study failed to complete the batterer intervention program, that number increased to 67 percent for those also required to complete drug treatment. For those required to complete drug treatment alone, the noncompletion rate was 60 percent. [183]

High rates of technical violations are common for probationers sentenced for domestic violence, including violations of no-contact orders and drug abstinence, and failure to attend batterer intervention programs. Various probation studies found technical violation (noncrime) rates ranging from 34 percent of those sentenced in the Brooklyn felony domestic violence court [164], 41 percent in Colorado [125], 61 percent in Champaign County, Ill. [109], and 25 to 44 percent in Rhode Island (regular vs. specialized domestic violence supervision). [141]

Implications for Prosecutors

Prosecutors should be reluctant to recommend court-ordered conditions including batterer intervention programs unless the violators are closely monitored and enforced. If prosecutors are involved in the enforcement process, and bringing violators back to court, they must commit the time and resources required to enforce compliance and hold violators accountable. (Research basis: Multiple studies from disparate jurisdictions across the country.)

Implications for Judges

Judges should take all appropriate steps to ensure that court conditions are enforced, violators are returned to court promptly, and violation cases (i.e., revocation hearings) are heard expeditiously. (Research basis: Multiple studies from disparate jurisdictions across the country.)

8.6   Do those who complete batterer programs do better than those who fail?

Abusers who complete batterer programs are less likely to reabuse than those who fail to attend, are noncompliant, or drop out. [9, 30, 48, 54, 87, 90, 183] The differences can be substantial.

A Chicago study of more than 500 court-referred batterers referred to 30 different programs found that recidivism after an average of 2.4 years was 14.3 percent for those who completed the program, whereas recidivism for those who did not complete the programs was more than twice that (34.6 percent). [12] Those who did not complete their program mandate in the Bronx court study were four times more likely to recidivate than those who completed their program. [183]

The multistate study of four programs found that abusers who completed the programs reduced their risk of reassault in a range of 46 to 66 percent. [86] A Florida study found that the odds that abusers who completed the program would be rearrested were half those of a control group not assigned to the program, whereas the odds of rearrest for those who failed to attend were two and one-half times higher than the control group. [60]

A Massachusetts study found that, over a six-year period, those who completed a certified batterer intervention program were significantly less likely to be rearraigned for any type of offense, a violent offense or a protection order violation. (Massachusetts does not have a domestic violence statute, so researchers could not differentiate domestic from nondomestic violence offenses.) The rate differences for these offenses, between those who completed a program and those who did not, was as follows: 47.7 vs. 83.6 percent for any crime, 33.7 vs. 64.2 percent for a violent crime, and 17.4 vs. 41.8 percent for violation of a protective order. [18] The Dallas study found that twice as many program dropouts as program completers were rearrested within 13 months: 39.7 vs. 17.9 percent for any charge, and 8.1 vs. 2.8 percent for assault arrests. [53] An Alexandria, Va., study of almost 2,000 domestic violence defendants found that noncompliance with court-ordered treatment was associated significantly with being a repeat offender. [172]

While some studies have found reduced reabuse for abusers who completed treatment programs, a few studies have found less dramatic reductions, for example, in Broward County, where the difference was only 4 percent vs. 5 percent [61], and in Brooklyn, where it was 16 percent vs. 26 percent. [205]

Implications for Prosecutors and Judges

Compliance with mandated batterer intervention programs provides prosecutors and judges with a dynamic risk instrument based on a defendant"s ongoing current behavior. Reabuse can be prevented if prosecutors and courts respond appropriately and expeditiously to batterers who fail to attend or to comply with court-referred batterer intervention programs. (Research basis: Multiple studies of batterer intervention programs in diverse jurisdictions across the country.)

8.7 Can court monitoring enhance batterer intervention program attendance?

Court monitoring can increase batterer intervention program attendance rates, specifically through periodic court compliance hearings. In the multistate evaluation of four different programs, researchers found that batterer intervention program completion rates rose from under 50 percent to 65 percent after a court introduced a mandatory appearance 30 days following imposition of a batterer intervention program mandate. [82] Similarly, implementation of a specialized domestic violence court in San Diego significantly increased attendance. Among other changes, the court instituted postdispositional compliance hearings. [180] Other domestic violence courts across the country have demonstrated completion rates of more than 50 percent, including the Brooklyn misdemeanor domestic violence court, where completion rates for batterers referred to two different batterer programs was documented at 68 and 77 percent. [31]

In a related finding, a large Massachusetts study found that those defendants ordered to attend programs as a condition of probation had a completion rate of 62 percent, whereas those ordered to attend without probation supervision had a completion rate of only 30 percent. [18] A Rhode Island study found that a specialized probation domestic violence supervision program more aggressively monitored and enforced program compliance, as measured by the number of violation hearings brought to court, than the state"s regular probation program involving officers with mixed caseloads. [141] A study of three domestic violence courts in Michigan, Wisconsin and Massachusetts found significantly increased offender compliance with batterer intervention programs, both in showing up and staying enrolled. All three courts featured postdispositional review hearings. [103]

Implications for Prosecutors and Judges

To increase program participation, prosecutors should recommend and judges should hold post-dispositional compliance hearings as well as placing abusers on supervised probation, even if their convictions were for misdemeanors or ordinance violations. (Research basis: Limited research has been conducted on this issue, but no research suggests that increased judicial monitoring does anything besides increasing batterers" attendance in the programs.

> **Performance Measure:** A 75-percent completion rate has been documented for batterers referred from the Circuit Court of Cook County (Chicago) to 30 area batterer intervention programs. (Research basis: A single study of 549 male domestic violence probationers who were referred to 30 area batterer intervention programs and completed them or were terminated at the time of the study. [12])

8.8 Which batterers are likely to fail to attend mandated batterer intervention treatment?

Researchers generally agree that there are a number of variables associated with failure to complete programs. They include being younger, having less education, having greater criminal histories and violence in their family of origin, being less often employed and less motivated to change, having substance abuse problems, having children, and lacking court sanctions for noncompliance. [15, 45, 46, 61, 86, 97, 98, 181, 194] A number of studies emphasize the positive correlation between program completion and "stakes in conformity," including the variables of age (being older), marital status (being married) and employment (being employed). [12, 61]

Studies also find that many of the same variables that predict noncompletion also predict reabuse or general recidivism. In the Florida probation study, an examination of court-referred batterers found that the same characteristics that predicted rearrest (including prior criminal history and stakes in conformity) also predicted missing at least one court-mandated program session. [61] Other studies, including a study of two Brooklyn batterer intervention programs, also found that employment correlated both positively with completion and negatively with rearrest. [31]

However, prior criminal history remains the strongest and most consistent predictor of noncompletion and new arrests. In the Brooklyn study, defendants with a prior arrest history were found to be four times more likely to fail to complete programs than defendants without prior arrests. [31] The Bronx court study similarly found that prior arrests as well as a history of drug abuse predicted both noncompletion and recidivism and found background demographics to be less important. [183]

Implications for Prosecutors and Judges

Screening referrals based on the common variables found to correlate with successful completion — age, prior criminal history and substance abuse — can reduce program failure. Alternatively, supplemental conditions targeting abusers with these characteristics may be necessary to assure successful program participation. (Research basis: Although not all studies find the same array of variables that predict program completion, reabuse and/or general recidivism, almost all of them find overlapping variables of age, prior criminal history and substance abuse.)

8.9 When are noncompliant abusers likely to drop out of batterer programs?

Several studies have found that batterers who do not complete batterer intervention programs are likely to be noncompliant from the start. Furthermore, these studies found that noncompliance at the first court monitoring predicted both program failure and recidivism. In the Brooklyn study, the strongest predictor of program failure was early noncompliance. Defendants who had not enrolled in a program by the time of their first compliance hearing were significantly less likely to complete the program than those enrolled by the first hearing. [31] These findings are similar to those found in the Bronx study. Defendants who were not in compliance at their first monitoring appearance were six times more likely to fail to complete the program than those in compliance at that time. [183]

These findings are consistent with extensive research indicating that the largest proportion of court-identified abusers who reabuse are likely to reabuse sooner rather than later. (See question, "When are abusers likely to reabuse?")

Implications for Prosecutors and Judges

To safeguard victims and/or new partners, prosecutors and courts should respond immediately to an abuser's first failure to enroll in or attend a court-mandated batterer intervention program. (Research basis: Although most studies do not report when noncompliant abusers failed their programs, the consistent findings among abusers referred to multiple programs, utilized by two different courts in New York, strongly support their findings.)

8.10 What should the prosecutor's response be if court-referred abusers are noncompliant with programs?

The Rhode Island probation study that compared probationers in specialized probation supervision caseloads with those in less stringent general caseloads found that the former committed significantly less reabuse over one year. The difference, however, applied only to what researchers called "lower risk" probationers, those without prior arrest histories. Although there were several differences in how the two caseloads were supervised, enforcement of batterer intervention program attendance was one of the major differences. The specialized group's program was more rigidly enforced, as measured by significantly more violations for nonattendance. As a result of the court violation hearings, most of the noncompliant probationers were required to attend weekly compliance court sessions until they completed the program. [141]

An evaluation of two model domestic violence courts found that victims in the court with significantly more probation revocations for noncompliance (12 percent vs. only 1 percent in the other court) reported significantly less reabuse than in the comparison court. In the court with more revocations, victims reported a lower frequency of physical assaults for up to 11 months after the study incident. The defendants in the court with the higher revocation rates had a significantly higher number of prior arrests than the defendants in the comparison court (8.3 vs. 3.7 percent). Researchers posited that lower domestic violence arrests were obtained primarily through early detection and incarceration of probationers who either continued to reabuse or failed to comply with conditions. [103]

Broward County probation study researchers concluded the following correlation between program noncompliance and reabuse: If abusers are not afraid of violating their court orders, they are also not afraid of the consequences of committing new offenses. [60]

Implications for Prosecutors

Prosecutors should recommend increased sanctions for noncompliant abusers. Incarceration will assure immediate victim protection at least for the length of the incarceration. Short of this, increased surveillance may be effective at reducing risk of reabuse for lower risk abusers. (Research basis: Multiple studies have found that doing nothing in regard to noncompliant, court-referred abusers results in significantly higher rates of reabuse. Two studies involving jurisdictions across four states suggest that vigorous enforcement of conditions is the key in deterring reabuse.)

8.11 What should the judge's response be if court-referred abusers are noncompliant with programs?

Among lower risk abusers on probation for domestic violence, one study cited increased enforcement of batterer program compliance (as indicated by significantly more violators brought into court by probation officers for noncompliance) as one major factor correlating with reduced reabuse over a two-year period. This was compared to a control group of probationers who were also referred to batterer intervention programs but were not monitored as rigorously or brought back to court because of noncompliance. As a result of court violation hearings, most noncompliant probationers were required to attend weekly compliance court sessions until they completed the program. Lower risk abusers included those who had not previously been probated for domestic violence. In addition to attending more revocation hearings, these probationers had slightly more contact with probation officers, officers attempted to contact victims at least once, and the probation officers supervised specialized domestic violence caseloads. [141]

An evaluation of two model domestic violence courts found that victims in the court with significantly more probation revocations for noncompliance (12 percent vs. only 1 percent in the other court) reported significantly less reabuse than in a comparison court. Victims from the other model court reported no difference with victims in a comparison court. In the court with more revocations, victims reported a lower frequency of physical assaults up to 11 months after the study incident. The defendants in the court with the high revocation rate had a significantly higher number of prior arrests than defendants in the comparison court (8.3 percent vs. 3.7 percent). Researchers posited that lower domestic violence arrests were obtained primarily through the early detection and incarceration of probationers who either continued to reabuse or failed to comply with conditions. [103]

Broward County probation study researchers concluded the following correlation between program noncompliance and reabuse: If abusers are not afraid of violating their court orders, they are also not afraid of the consequences of committing new offenses. [60]

Implications for Judges

Judges should respond to noncompliant abusers immediately to safeguard victims. (Research basis: Multiple studies have found that doing nothing with regard to noncompliant, court-referred abusers results in significantly higher rates of reabuse. Two studies involving jurisdictions across four states suggest that vigorous enforcement of conditions is the key in deterring reabuse.)

8.12 What should the prosecutor's or judge's response be to abusers who reoffend while enrolled or after completing a batterer intervention program?

Batterers rearrested while enrolled or after completing a batterer intervention program are at high risk for reabusing (also see question, "How many abusers are likely to do it again?"). The multistate batterer intervention program study found that the majority of court-referred batterers who reassaulted did so more than once. [84] Similarly, a Rhode Island probation study found that batterers who were arrested for domestic violence while their prior arrest was still pending, or while they were still on probation for an earlier offense (domestic or nondomestic), had the highest reabuse rates of any probated abuser, averaging over 50 percent. [141]

Implications for Prosecutors and Judges

Prosecutors should recommend incarceration, and judges should incarcerate, any offenders who reabuse while enrolled in batterer programs or after having completed the programs. Due to their limited "treatment effect," simply re-enrolling high-risk abusers in these programs endangers victims. Those abusers who reabuse are likely to continue doing so if left on their own. (Research basis: Both batterer program studies and general studies of court-identified batterers have found that repeatedly arrested abusers are chronic in their abusive behavior.)

8.13 What effect do batterer intervention program referrals have on victims?

Studies find that most victims are satisfied with their abuser"s referral to a batterer intervention program. In the Bronx study, 77 percent of victims were satisfied with the case outcome if the abuser was ordered to attend a program, compared to only 55 percent of victims who were satisfied when the abuser was not required to attend a program. [145] A survey of victims of men attending batterer intervention programs throughout Rhode Island found most female victims enthusiastic about the batterer programs. Some victims who were enthusiastic were reassaulted but still felt that the program improved their situation. [140] Program enrollment may also influence victims to remain with their abusers. Victims are more likely to remain with their abusers if their abusers are in treatment programs and are hopeful that the abusers will "get better." [58, 81]

Implications for Prosecutors and Judges

Prosecutors, judges, other court personnel and batterer intervention programs should warn victims that batterers" attendance at these programs does not ensure the cessation of abuse during or after the program. (Research basis: Consistent findings of victim surveys in multiple settings across the country as well as a control study of victims whose abusers were not sent to a batterer program.)

> **Bottom Line:** On the whole, unless batterer intervention programs are closely monitored and program compliance is rigorously enforced, batterer intervention programs may be ineffective and give false hope to victims.

References

1. Adams, D. *Why Do They Kill? Men Who Murder Their Intimate Partners.* Nashville, TN: Vanderbilt University Press, 2007.

2. Adams, S. *Serial Batterers.* Boston, MA: Office of the Commissioner of Probation, 1999.

3. Albucher, R., and I. Liberzon. "Psychopharmacological Treatment in PTSD: A Critical Review." *Journal of Psychiatric Research* 36(6) (2002): 355-367.

4. Aldarondo, E. "Evaluating the Efficacy of Interventions With Men Who Batter." In *Programs for Men Who Batter,* ed. E. Aldarondo and F. Mederos. Kingston, NJ: Civic Research Institute, 2002: 3-12.

5. Apsler, R., M. Cummins, and S. Carl. "Perceptions of the Police by Female Victims of Domestic Partner Violence." *Violence Against Women* 9(11) (November 2003): 1318-1335, NCJ 202666. http://www.ncjrs.gov/App/publications/abstract.aspx?ID=202666

6. Arias, I., and K. Pape. "Psychological Abuse: Implications for Adjustment and Commitment to Leave Violent Partners." *Violence and Victims* 14(1) (Spring 1999): 55-67.

7. Austin, J., and J. Dankwort. *A Review of Standards for Batterer Intervention Programs.* VAWnet Applied Research Forum, National Online Resource Center on Violence Against Women, revised August 1998, available online at http://new.vawnet.org/Assoc_Files_VAWnet/AR_standards.pdf

8. Babcock, J., C. Green, and C. Robie. "Does Batterers" Treatment Work? A Meta-Analytic Review of Domestic Violence Treatment." *Clinical Psychology Review* 23(8) (January 2004): 1023-1053.

9. Babcock, J., and R. Steiner. "The Relationship Between Treatment, Incarceration, and Recidivism of Battering: A Program Evaluation of Seattle"s Coordinated Community Response to Domestic Violence." *Journal of Family Psychology* 13(1) (March 1999): 46-59.

10. Bass, A., P. Nealon, and C. Armstrong. "The War on Domestic Abuse." *Boston Globe*, September 25, 1994, quoted in A. Klein, *The Criminal Justice Response to Domestic Violence.* Belmont, CA: Thomson/Wadsworth, 2004: 138.

11. Belknap, J., D. Graham, J. Hartman, V. Lippen, G. Allen, and J. Sutherland. "Factors Related to Domestic Violence Court Dispositions in a Large Urban Area: The Role of Victim/Witness Reluctance and Other Variables." Executive summary for National Institute of Justice, grant number 96-WT-NX-0004. Washington, DC: U.S. Department of Justice, National Institute of Justice, August 2000, NCJ 184112. http://www.ncjrs.gov/App/Publications/abstract.aspx?ID=184112

12. Bennett, L., C. Stoops, C. Call, and H. Flett. "Program Completion and Re-Arrest in a Batterer Intervention System." *Research on Social Work Practice*, 17(42) (2007): 42-54.

13. Benson, M., and G. Fox. "Concentrated Disadvantage, Economic Distress, and Violence Against Women in Intimate Relationships." Final report for National Institute of Justice, grant number 98-WT-VX-0011. Washington, DC: U.S. Department of Justice, National Institute of Justice, 2004, NCJ 199709.
http://www.ncjrs.gov/App/Publications/abstract.aspx?ID=199709

14. Benson, M., J. Wooldredge, A. Thistlethwaite, and G. Fox. "The Correlation Between Race and Domestic Violence Is Confounded in Community Context." *Social Problems* 51(3) (July 2004): 326-342.

15. Bersani, C., and H. Chen. "Sociological Perspectives in Family Violence." In *Handbook on Family Violence,* ed. V. Van Hasselt, R. Morrison, A. Bellack, and M. Hersen. New York: Plenum Press, 1988: 57-84.

16. Bible, A., and A. Weigl. "Cries of Abuse Unheeded, Assaults Rise to Murders." *News and Observer* [Raleigh, NC], May 18-20, 2003, quoted in A. Klein, *The Criminal Justice Response to Domestic Violence.* Belmont, CA: Thomson/Wadsworth, 2004: 139.

17. Block, C. "Risk Factors for Death or Life-Threatening Injury for Abused Women in Chicago." Final report for National Institute of Justice, grant number 96-IJ-CX-0020. Washington, DC: U.S. Department of Justice, National Institute of Justice, 2004, NCJ 199732.
http://www.ncjrs.gov/App/Publications/abstract.aspx?ID=199732

18. Bocko, S., C. Cicchetti, L. Lempicki, and A. Powell. *Restraining Order Violators, Corrective Programming and Recidivism.* Boston, MA: Office of the Commissioner of Probation, November 2004.

19. Brookoff, D. *Drugs, Alcohol, and Domestic Violence in Memphis.* Research Review. Washington, DC: U.S. Department of Justice, National Institute of Justice, October 1997, FS 000172.

20. Brundrett, R., and C. Roberts. "Domestic Abuse Cases Go to State." *The State* [Columbia, SC], July 12, 2001, quoted in A. Klein, *The Criminal Justice Response to Domestic Violence.* Belmont, CA: Thomson/Wadsworth, 2004: 139.

21. Brundrett, R., C. Roberts, and C. Leblanc. "S.C. Dismisses 54 Percent of Worst Domestic Violence Cases," *The State* [Columbia, SC], May 20, 2001, quoted in A. Klein, *The Criminal Justice Response to Domestic Violence.* Belmont, CA: Thomson/Wadsworth, 2004: 139.

22. Buzawa, E., and C. Buzawa, eds. *Domestic Violence: The Changing Criminal Justice Response.* Westport, CT: Auburn House, 1992.

23. Buzawa, E., G. Hotaling, A. Klein, and J. Byrnes. "Response to Domestic Violence in a Pro-Active Court Setting." Final report for National Institute of Justice, grant number 95-IJ-CX-0027. Washington, DC: U.S. Department of Justice, National Institute of Justice, July 1999, NCJ 181427.
http://www.ncjrs.gov/App/Publications/abstract.aspx?ID=181427

24. Campbell, J., C. O'Sullivan, J. Roehl, and D. Webster. "Intimate Partner Violence Risk Assessment Validation Study." Final report for National Institute for Justice, grant number 2000-WT-VX-0011. Washington, DC: U.S. Department of Justice, National Institute of Justice, May 2005 (rev. Dec. 2005), NCJ 209731.
http://www.ncjrs.gov/App/Publications/abstract.aspx?ID=209731

25. Campbell, J., D. Webster, J. Koziol-McLain, C. Block, D. Campbell, M. Curry, F. Gary, J. McFarlane, C. Sachs, P. Sharps, Y. Ulrich, and S. Wilt. "Assessing Risk Factors for Intimate Partner Homicide." *NIJ Journal* 250 (November 2003): 14-19, NCJ 196547.
http://www.ncjrs.gov/App/Publications/abstract.aspx?ID=196547

26. Carlson, M., S. Harris, and G. Holden. "Protective Orders and Domestic Violence: Risk Factors for Reabuse." *Journal of Family Violence* 14(2) (1999): 205-226.

27. Catalano, S. *Intimate Partner Violence in the United States.* Washington, DC: U.S. Department of Justice, Bureau of Justice Statistics, December 2007, available online at http://www.ojp.usdoj.gov/bjs/intimate/ipv.htm.

28. Cavanaugh, M., and R. Gelles. "The Utility of Male Domestic Violence Typologies. *Journal of Interpersonal Violence* 20(2) (2005): 155-166.

29. Chase, K. K. O'Leary, and R. Heyman. "Categorizing Partner-Violent Men Within the Reactive-Proactive Typology Model." *Journal of Consulting and Clinical Psychology* 69 (2001): 567-572.

30. Chen, H., C. Bersani, S. Myers, and R. Denton. "Evaluating the Effectiveness of a Court Sponsored Abuser Treatment Program." *Journal of Family Violence* 4(4) (December 1989): 309-322, NCJ 122317.
http://www.ncjrs.gov/App/Publications/abstract.aspx?ID=122317

31. Cissner, A., and N. Puffett. "Do Batterer Program Length or Approach Affect Completion or Re-Arrest Rates? A Comparison of Outcomes Between Defendants Sentenced to Two Batterer Programs in Brooklyn." New York, NY: Center for Court Innovation, September 2006, available online at
http://www.courtinnovation.org/_uploads/documents/IDCC_DCAP percent20final.pdf.

32. Cochran, D., S. Adams, and P. O'Brien. "From Chaos to Clarity in Understanding Domestic Violence." *Domestic Violence Report* 3(5) (June/July 1998): 65.

33. Cohen, R. *Probation and Parole Violators in State Prison, 1991.* Bureau of Justice Statistics Special Report. Washington, DC: U.S. Department of Justice, Bureau of Justice Statistics, August 1995, NCJ 149076.
http://www.ncjrs.gov/App/Publications/abstract.aspx?ID=149076

34. Collins, J., D. Spencer, J. Snodgrass, and S. Wheeless. "Linkage of Domestic Violence and Substance Abuse Services." Final report for National Institute of Justice, grant number 97-IJ-CX-0009. Washington, DC: U.S. Department of Justice, National Institute of Justice, May 1999, NCJ 194123.
http://www.ncjrs.gov/App/Publications/abstract.aspx?ID=194123

35. Dalton, B. "Batterer Characteristics and Treatment Completion." *Journal of Interpersonal Violence* 16(12) (2001): 1223-1238.

36. Daly, J., and S. Pelowski. "Predictors of Dropout Among Men Who Batter: A Review of Studies With Implications for Research and Practice." *Violence and Victims* 15(2) (Summer 2000): 137-160, NCJ 186644.
http://www.ncjrs.gov/App/Publications/abstract.aspx?ID=186644

37. Davis, R., and C. Maxwell. "Preventing Repeat Incidents of Family Violence: A Reanalysis of Data From Three Field Tests." Final report for National Institute of Justice, grant number 2000-WT-VX-0007. Washington, DC: U.S. Department of Justice, National Institute of Justice, July 2002, NCJ 200608.
http://www.ncjrs.gov/App/Publications/abstract.aspx?ID=200608

38. Davis, R., and B. Smith. "Domestic Violence Reforms: Empty Promises or Fulfilled Expectations?" *Crime and Delinquency* 41(4) (October 1995): 541-552, NCJ 157478.
http://www.ncjrs.gov/App/Publications/abstract.aspx?ID=157478

39. Davis, R., B. Smith, and L. Nickles. "The Deterrent Effect of Prosecuting Domestic Violence Misdemeanors." *Crime and Delinquency* 44(3) (July 1998): 434-442, NCJ 173568.
http://www.ncjrs.gov/App/Publications/abstract.aspx?ID=173568

40. Davis, R., B. Smith, and C. Rabbitt. "Increasing Convictions in Domestic Violence Cases: A Field Test in Milwaukee." *Justice System Journal* 22(1) (2001): 61-72, NCJ 188067.
http://www.ncjrs.gov/App/Publications/abstract.aspx?ID=188067

41. Davis, R., and B. Taylor. "A Proactive Response to Family Violence: The Results of a Randomized Experiment." *Criminology* 35(2) (May 1997): 307-333.

42. Davis, R., B. Taylor, and C. Maxwell. "Does Batterer Treatment Reduce Violence? A Randomized Experiment in Brooklyn." Final report to National Institute of Justice, grant number 94-IJ-CX-0047. Washington, DC: U.S. Department of Justice, National Institute of Justice, January 2000, NCJ 180772.
http://www.ncjrs.gov/App/Publications/abstract.aspx?ID=180772

43. Dawson, M., and R. Dinovitzer. "Victim Cooperation and the Prosecution of Domestic Violence in a Specialized Court." *Justice Quarterly* 18(3) (September 2001): 593-622, NCJ 190492. http://www.ncjrs.gov/App/Publications/abstract.aspx?ID=190492

44. de Becker, G. *The Gift of Fear*. Boston, MA: Little, Brown & Co., 1997, NCJ 177216.
http://www.ncjrs.gov/App/Publications/abstract.aspx?ID=177216

45. DeHart, D., R. Kennerly, L. Burke, and D. Follingstad. "Predictors of Attrition in a Treatment Program for Battering Men." *Journal of Family Violence* 14(1) (March 1999): 19-34, NCJ 177795.
http://www.ncjrs.gov/App/Publications/abstract.aspx?ID=177795

46. DeMaris, A. "Attrition in Batterers" Counseling: The Role of Social and Demographic Factors." *Social Review* 63 (1989): 142-154.

47. Deschner, J., J. McNeil, and M. Moore. "A Treatment Model for Batterers." *Social Casework* 67(1) (1986): 55-60, NCJ 105256.
http://www.ncjrs.gov/App/Publications/abstract.aspx?ID=105256

48. Dobash, R., R. Dobash, K. Cavanagh, and R. Lewis. "Reeducation Programmes for Violent Men: An Evaluation." *Research Findings* 46 (October 1996): 1-4.

49. Dugan, L., D. Nagin, and R. Rosenfeld. "Effects of State and Local Domestic Violence Policy on Intimate Partner Homicide." Final report for National Institute of Justice, grant number 97-WT-VX-0004. Washington, DC: U.S. Department of Justice, National Institute of Justice, 2004, NCJ 199711.
http://www.ncjrs.gov/App/publications/abstract.aspx?ID=202666

50. Dunford, F. "System Initiated Warrants for Suspects of Misdemeanor Domestic. Assault: A Pilot Study." *Justice Quarterly* 7(4) (1990): 631-653.

51. Dunford, F. "The San Diego Navy Experiment: An Assessment of Interventions for Men Who Assault Their Wives." *Journal of Consulting and Clinical Psychology* 68(3) (2000): 468-476.

52. Eckberg, D., and M. Podkopacz. "Domestic Violence Court in Minneapolis: Three Levels of Analysis." Presentation at American Society of Criminologists annual meeting, Chicago, IL, November 15, 2002.

53. Eckhardt, C. "Stages and Processes of Change and Associated Treatment Outcomes in Partner Assaultive Men." Final report for National Institute of Justice, grant number 99-WT-VX-0012. Washington, DC: U.S. Department of Justice, National Institute of Justice, August 2003, NCJ 205022.
http://www.ncjrs.gov/App/Publications/abstract.aspx?ID=205022

54. Edleson, J., and R. Grusznski. "Treating Men Who Batter: Four Years of Outcome Data from the Domestic Abuse Project." *Journal of Social Service Research* 12(3) (1988): 3-22.

55. Fagan, J., E. Friedman, S. Wexler, and V. Lewis. *The National Family Violence Program: Final Evaluation Report.* San Francisco, CA: URSA Institute, 1984.

56. Fals-Stewart, W. (2003). "The Occurrence of Partner Physical Aggression on Days of Alcohol Consumption: A Longitudinal Diary Study." *Journal of Consulting Psychology* 71(1): 41-52.

57. Family Violence Project. "Family Violence: Improving Court Practice." *Juvenile and Family Court Journal* 41(4) (1990): 14-15, NCJ 131619.
http://www.ncjrs.gov/App/Publications/abstract.aspx?ID=131619

58. Feazell, C., R. Mayers, and J. Deschner. "Services for Men Who Batter: Implications for Programs and Policies." *Family Relations* 33(2) (April 1984): 217-223.

59. Feder, L. "Police Handling of Domestic Violence Calls: An Overview and Further Investigation." *Women and Criminal Justice* 10(2) (1999): 49-68, NCJ 177884.
http://www.ncjrs.gov/App/Publications/abstract.aspx?ID=177884

60. Feder, L., and L. Dugan. "Testing a Court-Mandated Treatment Program for Domestic Violence Offenders: The Broward Experiment." Final report for National Institute of Justice, grant number 96-WT-NX-0008. Washington, DC: U.S. Department of Justice, National Institute of Justice, 2004, NCJ 199729.
http://www.ncjrs.gov/App/Publications/abstract.aspx?ID=199729

61. Feder, L., and D. Forde. "A Test of the Efficacy of Court-Mandated Counseling for Domestic Violence Offenders: The Broward Experiment." Final report for National Institute of Justice, grant number 96-WT-NX-0008. Washington, DC: U.S. Department of Justice, National Institute of Justice, June 2000, NCJ 184752.
http://www.ncjrs.gov/App/Publications/abstract.aspx?ID=184752

62. Feder, L., and D. Wilson. "A Meta-Analytic Review of Court-Mandated Batterer Intervention Programs: Can Courts Affect Abusers" Behaviors?" *Journal of Experimental Criminology* 1(2) (July 2005): 239-262.

63. Felson, R., J. Ackerman, and C. Gallagher. "Police Intervention and the Repeat of Domestic Assault." Final report for National Institute of Justice, grant number 2002-WG-BX-2002. Washington, DC: U.S. Department of Justice, National Institute of Justice, June 2005, NCJ 210301.
http://www.ncjrs.gov/App/Publications/abstract.aspx?ID=210301

64. Finn, M. "Effects of Victims" Experiences With Prosecutors on Victim Empowerment and Re-Occurrence of Intimate Partner Violence." Final report for National Institute of Justice, grant number 99-WT-VX-0008. Washington, DC: U.S. Department of Justice, National Institute of Justice, August 2003, NCJ 202983.
http://www.ncjrs.gov/App/Publications/abstract.aspx?ID=202983

65. Finn, M., B. Blackwell, L. Stalans, S. Studdard, and. L. Dugan. "Dual Arrest Decisions in Domestic Violence Cases: The Influence of Departmental Policies." *Crime and Delinquency* 50(4) (October 2004): 565-589, NCJ 207463.
http://www.ncjrs.gov/App/Publications/abstract.aspx?ID=207463

66. Ford, D., and M.J. Regoli. "The Preventive Impacts of Policies for Prosecuting Wife Batterers." In *Domestic Violence: The Changing Criminal Justice Response,* eds. E. Buzawa and C. Buzawa. Westport, CT: Auburn House, 1992: 181-208.

67. Ford, D., and M.J. Regoli. "The Indianapolis Domestic Violence Prosecution Experiment." Final report for National Institute of Justice, grant number 86-IJ-CX-0012, and National Institute of Mental Health/DHHS, grant number MH-15161-13. Washington, DC: U.S. Department of Justice, National Institute of Justice, 1993, NCJ 157870.
http://www.ncjrs.gov/App/Publications/abstract.aspx?ID=157870

68. Friday, P., V. Lord, M. Exum, and J. Hartman. "Evaluating the Impact of a Specialized Domestic Violence Police Unit." Final report for National Institute of Justice, grant number

2004-WG-BX-0004. Washington, DC: U.S. Department of Justice, National Institute of Justice, May 2006, NCJ 215916.
http://www.ncjrs.gov/App/Publications/abstract.aspx?ID=237505

69. Gamache, D., J. Edleson, and M. Schock. "Coordinated Police, Judicial and Social Services Response to Woman Battering: A Multiple-Baseline Evaluation Across Three Communities." In *Coping With Family Violence: Research and Policy Perspectives,* ed. G. Hotaling, D. Finkelhor, J. Kirkpatrick. and M. Straus. Beverly Hills, CA: Sage, 1988: 193-211, NCJ 114456.
http://www.ncjrs.gov/App/Publications/abstract.aspx?ID=114456

70. Garner, J. "What Does „the Prosecution" of Domestic Violence Mean?" *Criminology and Public Policy* 4(3) (August 2005): 567-573.

71. Garner, J., and C. Maxwell. *Prosecution and Conviction Rates for Intimate Partner Violence.* Shepherdstown, WV: Joint Centers for Justice Studies, 2008: 49.

72. Gelles, R. *Intimate Violence in Families* (3rd ed.). Thousand Oaks, CA: Sage, 1997.

73. Giacomazzi, A., and M. Smithey. "Collaborative Effort Toward Resolving Family Violence Against Women." Final report for National Institute of Justice, grant number 97-WE-VX-0131. Washington, DC: U.S. Department of Justice, National Institute of Justice, 2004, NCJ 199716.
http://www.ncjrs.gov/App/Publications/abstract.aspx?ID=199716

74. Gist, J., J. McFarlane, A. Malecha, N. Fredland, P. Schultz, and P. Willson. "Women in Danger: Intimate Partner Violence Experienced by Women That Qualify and Do Not Qualify for a Protective Order." *Behavioral Sciences and the Law* 19(5-6) (January 9, 2002): 637-647.

75. Gist, J., J. McFarlane, A. Malecha, P. Willson, K. Watson, N. Fredland, P. Schultz, T. Walsh, I. Hall, and S. Smith. "Protection Orders and Assault Charges: Do Justice Interventions Reduce Violence Against Women?" *American Journal of Family Law* 15(1) (2001): 59-71.

76. Gleason, W. "Mental Disorders in Battered Women: An Empirical Study." *Violence and Victims* 8(1) (Spring 1993): 53-68, NCJ 148472.
http://www.ncjrs.gov/App/Publications/abstract.aspx?ID=148472

77. Golding J. "Intimate Partner Violence as a Risk Factor for Mental Disorders: A Meta-Analysis." *Journal of Family Violence* 14(2) (June 1999): 99-132, NCJ 178109.
http://www.ncjrs.gov/App/Publications/abstract.aspx?ID=178109

78. Goldkamp, J. "The Role of Drug and Alcohol Abuse in Domestic Violence and Its Treatment: Dade County"s Domestic Violence Court Experiment." Final report for National Institute of Justice, grant number 93-IJ-CX-0028. Washington, DC: U.S. Department of Justice, National Institute of Justice, 1996, NCJ 163410.
http://www.ncjrs.gov/App/Publications/abstract.aspx?ID=163410

79. Goldkamp, J., D. Weiland, M. Collins, and M. White. "The Role of Drug and Alcohol Abuse in Domestic Violence and Its Treatment: Dade County's Domestic Violence Court Experiment." Appendices to the final report for National Institute of Justice, grant number 93-IJ-CX-0028. Washington, DC: U.S. Department of Justice, National Institute of Justice, 1996, NCJ 163408.
http://www.ncjrs.gov/App/Publications/abstract.aspx?ID=163408

80. Gondolf, E. "How Some Men Stop Battering: An Evaluation of a Group Counseling Program." Paper presented at Second National Conference on Family Violence, Durham, NH, August 1984, and cited in E. Gondolf and D Russell, "The Case Against Anger Control Treatment Programs for Batterers," . Response to the Victimization of Women & Children 9(3) (1986): 2-5.

81. Gondolf, E. "Evaluating Programs for Men Who Batter: Problems and Prospects." Journal of Family Violence 2(1) (March 1987): 95-108, NCJ 105396.
http://www.ncjrs.gov/App/Publications/abstract.aspx?ID=105396

82. Gondolf, E. The Impact of Mandatory Court Review on Batterer Program Compliance: An Evaluation of the Pittsburgh Municipal Courts and Domestic Violence Abuse Counseling Center (DACC), Final Report. Harrisburg, PA: Pennsylvania Commission on Crime and Delinquency, May 15, 1997, NCJ 214567.
http://www.ncjrs.gov/App/Publications/abstract.aspx?ID=236118

83. Gondolf, E. "Patterns of Reassault in Batterer Programs." Violence and Victims 12(4) (Winter 1997): 373-388, NCJ 173329.
http://www.ncjrs.gov/App/Publications/abstract.aspx?ID=173329

84. Gondolf, E. Multi-Site Evaluation of Batterer Intervention Systems: A 30-Month Follow-Up of Court-Mandated Batterers in Four Cities. Brief Report. Indiana, PA: Mid-Atlantic Addiction Research and Training Institute, August 18, 1998, NCJ 183367.
http://www.ncjrs.gov/App/Publications/abstract.aspx?ID=183367

85. Gondolf, E. "30-Month Follow-Up of Court-Referred Batterers in Four Cities." International Journal of Offender Therapy and Comparative Criminology 44(1) (February 2000): 111-128, NCJ 181487.
http://www.ncjrs.gov/App/Publications/abstract.aspx?ID=181487

86. Gondolf, E. Batterer Intervention Systems. Thousand Oaks, CA: Sage, 2002.

87. Gondolf, E. "Culturally-Focused Batterer Counseling for African-American Men." Final report for National Institute of Justice, grant number 2001-WT-BX-0003. Washington, DC: U.S. Department of Justice, National Institute of Justice, June 10, 2005, NCJ 210828.
http://www.ncjrs.gov/App/Publications/abstract.aspx?ID=210828

88. Gondolf, E., and A. Jones. "The Program Effect of Batterer Programs in Three Cities." Violence and Victims 16(6) (December 2001): 693-704, NCJ 193654.
http://www.ncjrs.gov/App/Publications/abstract.aspx?ID=193654

89. Gondolf, E., and R. White. "Batterer Program Participants Who Repeatedly Reassault: Psychopathic Tendencies and Other Disorders." *Journal of Interpersonal Violence* 16(4) (April 2001): 361-380, NCJ 208765.
http://www.ncjrs.gov/App/Publications/abstract.aspx?ID=208765

90. Gordon, J., and L. Moriarty. "The Effects of Domestic Violence Batterer Treatment on Domestic Violence Recidivism: The Chesterfield County Experience." *Criminal Justice and Behavior: An International Journal* 30(1) (February 2003): 118-134, NCJ 198836.
http://www.ncjrs.gov/App/Publications/abstract.aspx?ID=198836

91. Gover, A., J. MacDonald, and G. Alpert. "Combating Domestic Violence: Findings From an Evaluation of a Local Domestic Violence Court." *Criminology and Public Policy* 3(1) (November 2003): 109-132, NCJ 203428.
http://www.ncjrs.gov/App/Publications/abstract.aspx?ID=203428

92. Grau, J., J. Fagan, and S. Wexler. "Restraining Orders for Battered Women: Issues of Access and Efficacy." In *Criminal Justice Politics and Women: The Aftermath of Legally Mandated Change*, ed. C. Schweber and C. Feinman. New York: Hawthorn Press, 1985: 13-28, NCJ 097703.
http://www.ncjrs.gov/App/Publications/abstract.aspx?ID=097703

93. Greenfeld, L., M. Rand, D. Craven, P. Klaus, C. Perkins, C. Ringel, G. Warchol, C. Maston, and J. Fox. *Violence by Intimates: Analysis of Data on Crimes by Current or Former Spouses, Boyfriends, and Girlfriends*. Factbook. Washington, DC: Bureau of Justice Statistics, March 1998, NCJ 167237.
http://www.ncjrs.gov/App/Publications/abstract.aspx?ID=167237

94. Greenfeld, L., and M. Zawitz. *Weapons Offenses and Offenders*. Bureau of Justice Statistics Selected Findings. Washington, DC: U.S. Department of Justice, Bureau of Justice Statistics, November 1995, NCJ 155284.
http://www.ncjrs.gov/App/Publications/abstract.aspx?ID=155284

95. Grisso, J., D. Schwarz, N. Hirschinger, M. Sammel, C. Brensinger, J. Santanna, R. Lowe, E. Anderson, L. Shaw, C. Bethel, and L. Teeple. "Violent Injuries Among Women in an Urban Area." *New England Journal of Medicine* 341(25) (December 16, 1999): 1899-1905.

96. Gross, M., E. Cramer, J. Forte, J. Gordon, T. Kunkel, and L. Moriarty. "The Impact of Sentencing Options on Recidivism Among Domestic Violence Offenders: A Case Study." *American Journal of Criminal Justice* 24(2) (Spring 2000): 301-312, NCJ 184477.
http://www.ncjrs.gov/App/Publications/abstract.aspx?ID=184477

97. Grusznski, R., and T. Carrillo. "Who Completes Batterers" Treatment Groups? An Empirical Investigation." *Journal of Family Violence* 3(2) (June 1988): 141-150.

98. Hamberger, K., and J. Hastings. "Skills Training for Treatment of Spouse Abusers: An Outcome Study." *Journal of Family Violence* 3(2) (June 1988): 121-130.

99. Hanson, R., and S. Wallace-Capretta. *A Multi-Site Study of Treatment for Abusive Men*. Report No. 2000-05. Ottawa, Ontario, Canada: Department of the Solicitor General Canada, 2000.

100. Hanson, R., and S. Wallace-Capretta. *Predicting Recidivism Among Male Batterers.* Report No. 2000-06. Ottawa, Ontario, Canada: Department of the Solicitor General Canada, 2000.

101. Hardeman, J. *Implementation of the Abuse Prevention Act (209A).* Waltham, MA: Heller School, Brandeis University, 1995.

102. Harrell, A. "Evaluation of a Court-Ordered Treatment for Domestic Violence Offenders." Final report for National Institute of Justice, grant number 90-12L-E-089. Washington, DC: U.S. Department of Justice, National Institute of Justice. and The Urban Institute, 1991, NCJ 139749.
http://www.ncjrs.gov/App/Publications/abstract.aspx?ID=139749

103. Harrell, A., J. Castro, L. Newmark, and C. Visher. "Final Report on the Evaluation of the Judicial Oversight Demonstration: Executive Summary." Final report for National Institute of Justice, grant number 99-WT-VX-K005. Washington, DC: U.S. Department of Justice, National Institute of Justice, and The Urban Institute, June 2007, NCJ 219386, available online at http://www.urban.org/publications/411498.html.

104. Harrell, A., M. Schaffer, C. DeStefano, and J. Castro. "The Evaluation of Milwaukee"s Judicial Oversight Demonstration." Final report for National Institute of Justice, grant number 99-WT-VX-K005. Washington, DC: U.S. Department of Justice, National Institute of Justice, and The Urban Institute, April 2006, available online at http://www.urban.org/publications/411315.html.

105. Harrell, A., and B. Smith. "Effects of Restraining Orders on Domestic Violence Victims." In *Do Arrest and Restraining Orders Work?* ed. E. Buzawa and C. Buzawa. Thousand Oaks, CA: Sage, 1996: 214-243.

106. Harrell, A., B. Smith, and L. Newmark. *Court Processing and the Effects of Restraining Orders for Domestic Violence Victims.* Washington, DC: Urban Institute, May 1, 1993, available online at http://www.urban.org/url.cfm?ID=405114.

107. Hartley, C., and L. Frohmann. "Cook County Target Abuser Call (TAC): An Evaluation of a Specialized Domestic Violence Court." Final report for National Institute of Justice, grant number 2000-WT-VX-0003. Washington, DC: U.S. Department of Justice, National Institute of Justice, August 2003, NCJ 202944.
http://www.ncjrs.gov/App/Publications/abstract.aspx?ID=202944

108. Hayler, B., and M. Addison-Lamb. "A Process and Implementation Evaluation of the Specialized Domestic Violence Probation Projects in Illinois"s Peoria, Sangamon, and Tazewell Counties." Springfield, IL: University of Illinois at Springfield, November 2000.

109. Hayler, B., N. Ford, and M. Addison-Lamb. "An Implementation Evaluation of the Enhanced Domestic Violence Probation Program in Champaign County." Final report for Bureau of Justice Assistance, grant number 96-DB-MU-0017. Washington, DC: U.S. Department of Justice, Bureau of Justice Assistance, December 1999, NCJ 188355.
http://www.ncjrs.gov/App/Publications/abstract.aspx?ID=188355

110. Healey, K. C. Smith, and C. O"Sullivan. *Batterer Intervention: Program Approaches and Criminal Justice Strategies.* NIJ Issues and Practices, February 1998, grant number OJP-94-C-007, NCJ 168638.
http://www.ncjrs.gov/App/Publications/abstract.aspx?ID=168638

111. Heckert, D., and E. Gondolf. "Assessing Assault Self-Reports by Batterer Program Participants and Their Partners." *Journal of Family Violence* 15(2) (June 2000): 181-197.

112. Heckert, D., and E. Gondolf. "Battered Women"s Perceptions of Risk Versus Risk Factors and Instruments in Predicting Repeat Reassault." *Journal of Interpersonal Violence* 19(7) (2004): 778-800.

113. Heckert, D., and E. Gondolf. "Do Multiple Outcomes and Conditional Factors Improve Prediction of Batterer Reassault?" *Violence and Victims* 20(1) (February 2005): 3-24, NCJ 210809.
http://www.ncjrs.gov/App/Publications/abstract.aspx?ID=210809

114. Hendricks, J., ed. *Crisis Intervention in Criminal Justice and Social Services.* Springfield, IL: Charles C Thomas Publishers, 1991.

115. Henning, K., and L. Klesges. *Evaluation of the Shelby County Domestic Violence Court.* Shelby County, TN: Shelby County Government, 1999.

116. Hilton, N., G. Harris, M. Rice, C. Lang, C. Cormier, and K. Lines. "A Brief Actuarial Assessment for the Prediction of Wife Assault Recidivism: The Ontario Domestic Assault Risk Assessment." *Psychological Assessment* 16(3) (September 2004): 267-275.

117. Hirschel, D., E. Buzawa, A. Pattavina, D. Faggiani, and M. Reuland. "Explaining the Prevalence, Context, and Consequences of Dual Arrest in Intimate Partner Cases." Final report for National Institute of Justice, grant number 2001-WT-BX-0501. Washington, DC: U.S. Department of Justice, National Institute of Justice, April 2007, NCJ 218355.
http://www.ncjrs.gov/App/Publications/abstract.aspx?ID=240055

118. Hirschel, J., and D. Dawson. "Violence Against Women: Synthesis of Research for Law Enforcement Officials." Final report for National Institute of Justice, grant number 98-WT-VX-K001. Washington, DC: U.S. Department of Justice, National Institute of Justice, December 2000, NCJ 198372.
http://www.ncjrs.gov/App/Publications/abstract.aspx?ID=198372

119. Hirschel, J., and I. Hutchison. "The Relative Effects of Offense, Offender, and Victim Variables on the Decision to Prosecute Domestic Violence Cases." *Violence Against Women* 7(1) (January 2001): 46-59, NCJ 186664.
http://www.ncjrs.gov/App/Publications/abstract.aspx?ID=186664

120. Holt, V., M. Kernic, T. Lumley, M. Wolf, and F. Rivara. "Civil Protection Orders and Risk of Subsequent Police-Reported Violence." *Journal of the American Medical Association* 288(5) (August 7, 2002): 589-594, NCJ 196566.
http://www.ncjrs.gov/App/Publications/abstract.aspx?ID=196566

121. Holt, V., M. Kernic, M. Wolf, and F. Rivara. "Do Protection Orders Affect the Likelihood of Future Partner Violence and Injury?" *American Journal of Preventive Medicine* 24(1) (2003): 16-21.

122. Holtzworth-Munroe, A., and J. Meehan. "Typologies of Men Who Are Maritally Violent: Scientific and Clinical Implications." *Journal of Interpersonal Violence* 19(12) (December 2004): 1369-1389.

123. Holtzworth-Munroe, A., and G. Stuart. "Typologies of Male Batterers: Three Subtypes and the Differences Among Them." *Psychological Bulletin* 116(3) (November 1994): 476-497.

124. Hotaling, G., and E. Buzawa. "Victim Satisfaction with Criminal Justice Case Processing in a Model Court Setting." Final report for National Institute of Justice, grant number 2000-WT-VX-0019. Washington, DC: U.S. Department of Justice, National Institute of Justice, January 2003, NCJ 195668.
http://www.ncjrs.gov/App/Publications/abstract.aspx?ID=195668

125. Huntley, S. and L. Kilzer. Battered Justice Series (4 parts). *Rocky Mountain News* [Denver,CO] (February 5, 7-9, 2005), available from
http://www.rockymountainnews.com/news/2005/feb/05/compassions-high-price/,
http://www.rockymountainnews.com/news/2005/Feb/07/span-classdeeplinksredsecond-in-a-seriesspanbr/, http://www.rockymountainnews.com/news/2005/Feb/08/span-classdeeplinksredbattered-justice-part-fast/, and
http://www.rockymountainnews.com/news/2005/feb/09/div-classdeeplinksredbattered-justice-part-4div/

126. Hutchison, I. "The Influence of Alcohol and Drugs on Women"s Utilization of the Police for Domestic Violence." Final report for National Institute of Justice, grant number 97-IJ-CX-0047. Washington, DC: U.S. Department of Justice, National Institute of Justice, June 1999, NCJ 179277.
http://www.ncjrs.gov/App/Publications/abstract.aspx?ID=179277

127. Isaac, N., and P. Enos. "Medical Records as Legal Evidence of Domestic Violence." Final report for National Institute of Justice, grant number 97-WT-VX-0008. Washington, DC: U.S. Department of Justice, National Institute of Justice, May 2000, NCJ 184528.
http://www.ncjrs.gov/App/Publications/abstract.aspx?ID=184528

128. Jacobson, N., and J. Gottman. *When Men Batter Women.* New York: Simon & Schuster, 1998.

129. Johannson, M., and L. Tutty. "An Evaluation of After-Treatment Couples' Groups for Wife Abuse." *Family Relations* 47(1) (January 1998): 27-35.

130. Jolin, A., W. Feyerherm, R. Fountain, and S. Friedman. "Beyond Arrest: The Portland, Oregon Domestic Violence Experiment." Final report for National Institute of Justice, grant number 95-IJ-CX-0054. Washington, DC: U.S. Department of Justice, National Institute of Justice, 1998, NCJ 179968.
http://www.ncjrs.gov/App/Publications/abstract.aspx?ID=179968

131. Jurik, N., and R. Winn. "Gender and Homicide: A Comparison of Men and Women Who Kill." *Violence and Victims* 5(4) (Winter 1990): 227-242, NCJ 130043.
http://www.ncjrs.gov/App/Publications/abstract.aspx?ID=130043

132. Keilitz, S. "Specialization of Domestic Violence Case Management in the Courts: A National Survey." Final report for National Institute of Justice, grant number 98-WT-VX-0002. Washington, DC: U.S. Department of Justice, National Institute of Justice, 2004, NCJ 199724.
http://www.ncjrs.gov/App/Publications/abstract.aspx?ID=199724

133. Keilitz, S., P. Hannaford, and H. Efkeman. "Civil Protection Orders: The Benefits and Limitations for Victims of Domestic Violence." Final report for National Institute of Justice, grant number 93-IJ-CX-0035. Washington, DC: U.S. Department of Justice, National Institute of Justice, 1997, NCJ 172223.
http://www.ncjrs.gov/App/Publications/abstract.aspx?ID=172223

134. Klein, A. "Re-Abuse in a Population of Court-Restrained Male Batterers: Why Restraining Orders Don't Work." In *Do Arrests and Restraining Orders Work?* ed. E. Buzawa and C. Buzawa. Thousand Oaks, CA: Sage, 1996: 192-214, NCJ 161527.
http://www.ncjrs.gov/App/Publications/abstract.aspx?ID=161527

135. Klein, A. *The Criminal Justice Response to Domestic Violence*. Belmont, CA: Thomson/Wadsworth, 2004.

136. Klein, A. *Rhode Island Domestic Violence Shelter and Advocacy Services: An Assessment.* Waltham, MA: BOTEC Analysis Corporation and Rhode Island Justice Commission, June 29, 2005, available online at http://www.rijustice.ri.gov/sac/Reports/Final%20ShelterEval%209-20-05.pdf. The Rhode Island arrests may include multiple arrests of the same suspects involving incidents with the same victims within that year. It should also be noted that Rhode Island mandates arrest for "domestic violence," which is defined broadly to include any crime committed by current or former intimate partners, family or household members, and dating partners, although most Rhode Island domestic violence arrests are, in fact, for simple assault.

137. Klein, A., and A. Crowe. (2008). "Findings From and Outcome Examination of Rhode Island"s Specialized Domestic Violence Probation Supervision Program: Do Specialized Supervision Programs of Batterers Reduce Reabuse?" *Violence Against Women* 14(2) (February 1, 2008): 226-246.

138. Klein, A., and T. Tobin. (2008). "Longitudinal Study of Arrested Batterers, 1995-2005: Career Criminals." *Violence Against Women* 14(2) (February 2008): 136-157, NCJ 221764.
http://www.ncjrs.gov/App/Publications/abstract.aspx?ID=243648

139. Klein, A., T. Tobin, A. Salomon, and J. Dubois. "A Statewide Profile of Abuse of Older Women and the Criminal Justice Response." Final report for National Institute of Justice, grant number 2006-WG-BX-0009, Washington, DC: U.S. Department of Justice, National Institute of Justice, December 2007, NCJ 222460.
http://www.ncjrs.gov/App/Publications/abstract.aspx?ID=244358

140. Klein, A., and D. Wilson. *A Victim Survey on the Effects of a Court-Mandated Batterer Intervention Program in Rhode Island.* Waltham, MA: BOTEC Analysis Corporation, April 21, 2003, available online at http://www.rijustice.state.ri.us/sac/Reports/BI percent20Program.pdf.

141. Klein, A., D. Wilson, A. Crowe, and M. DeMichele. "Evaluation of the Rhode Island Probation Specialized Domestic Violence Supervision Unit." Final report for National Institute of Justice, grant number 2002-WG-BX-0011, March 31, 2005, NCJ 222912. http://www.ncjrs.gov/App/Publications/abstract.aspx?ID=244821

142. Koziol-McLain, J., D. Webster, J. McFarlane, C. Block, Y. Ulrich, N. Glass, and J. Campbell. "Risk Factors for Femicide-Suicide in Abusive Relationships: Results From a Multisite Case Control Study." *Violence and Victims* 21(1) (February 2006): 3-21, NCJ 213274.
http://www.ncjrs.gov/App/Publications/abstract.aspx?ID=234770

143. Kramer, R. "Alcohol and Victimization Factors in the Histories of Abused Women Who Come to Court: A Retrospective Case-Control Study." Dissertation AAT 8923570. Ann Arbor, MI: UMI Dissertation Services, 1989.

144. Kyriacou, D., D. Anglin, E. Taliaferro, S. Stone, T. Tubb, J. Linden, R. Muelleman, E. Barton, and J. Kraus. "Risk Factors for Injury to Women From Domestic Violence." *New England Journal of Medicine* 341(25) (December 16, 1999): 1892-1898.

145. Labriola, M., M. Rempel, and R. Davis. "Testing the Effectiveness of Batterer Programs and Judicial Monitoring: Results From a Randomized Trial at the Bronx Misdemeanor Domestic Violence Court." Final report for National Institute of Justice, grant number 2001-WT-BX-0506. New York: Center for Court Innovation, National Institute of Justice, November 2005, available online at
http://www.courtinnovation.org/_uploads/documents/battererprogramseffectiveness.pdf.

146. Labriola, M., M. Rempel, C. O'Sullivan, and P. Frank, with J. McDowell and R. Finkelstein. "Court Responses to Batterer Program Noncompliance: A National Perspective." Final report for National Institute of Justice, grant number 2004-WG-BX-0005. New York: Center for Court Innovation, March 2007, available online at
http://www.courtinnovation.org/_uploads/documents/Court_Responses_March2007.pdf.

147. Lane, E., R. Greenspan, and D. Weisburd. "The Second Responders Program: A Coordinated Police and Social Service Response to Domestic Violence." Final report for National Institute of Justice, grant number 98-WT-VX-0001. Washington, DC: U.S. Department of Justice, National Institute of Justice, 2004, NCJ 199717.
http://www.ncjrs.gov/App/Publications/abstract.aspx?ID=199717

148. Lindquist, C., C. Telch, and J. Taylor. Evaluation of a Conjugal Violence Treatment Program: A Pilot Study." *Behavioral Counseling and Community Interventions* 3(1) (1983): 76-90.

149. Lockyer, B. *Domestic Violence: Keeping the Promise, Victim Safety and Batterer Accountability.* Report to the California Attorney General from the Task Force on Local Criminal Justice Response to Domestic Violence. Sacramento, CA: Office of the Attorney

General, June 2005, available online at
http://www.safestate.org/documents/DV_Report_AG.pdf.

150. Logan, T., L. Shannon, R. Walker, and T. Faragher. "Protective Orders: Questions and Conundrums." *Trauma, Violence and Abuse* 7(3) (July 2006): 175-205, NCJ 216026.
http://www.ncjrs.gov/App/Publications/abstract.aspx?ID=237623

151. Lyon, E. "Special Session Domestic Violence Courts: Enhanced Advocacy and Interventions, Final Report Summary." Final report for National Institute of Justice, grant number 98-WE-VX-0031. Washington, DC: U.S. Department of Justice, National Institute of Justice, October 2002, NCJ 197860.
http://www.ncjrs.gov/App/Publications/abstract.aspx?ID=197860

152. Lyon, E. "Impact Evaluation of Special Session Domestic Violence: Enhanced Advocacy and Interventions." Final report for National Institute of Justice, grant number 2000-WE-VX-0014. Washington, DC: U.S. Department of Justice, National Institute of Justice, April 2005, NCJ 210362.
http://www.ncjrs.gov/App/Publications/abstract.aspx?ID=210362

153. Macmillan, R., and C. Kruttschnitt. "Patterns of Violence Against Women: Risk Factors and Consequences." Final report for National Institute of Justice, grant number 2002-IJ-CX-0011. Washington, DC: U.S. Department of Justice, National Institute of Justice, August 2004, NCJ 208346.
http://www.ncjrs.gov/App/Publications/abstract.aspx?ID=208346

154. Malcoe, L., and B. Duran. "Intimate Partner Violence and Injury in the Lives of Low-Income Native American Women." Final report for National Institute on Drug Abuse and National Institutes of Health as part of Interagency Consortium on Violence Against Women and Violence Within the Family, including National Institute of Justice, grant number 5R03-DA/AA11154. Washington, DC: U.S. Department of Justice, National Institute of Justice, 2004, NCJ 199703. http://www.ncjrs.gov/App/Publications/abstract.aspx?ID=199703

155. Maxwell, C., J. Garner, and J. Fagan. *The Effects of Arrest on Intimate Partner Violence: New Evidence From the Spouse Assault Replication Program.* Research in Brief. Washington, DC: U.S. Department of Justice, National Institute of Justice, July 2001, NCJ 188199.
http://www.ncjrs.gov/App/Publications/abstract.aspx?ID=188199

156. McFarlane, J., J. Campbell, and S. Wilt. "Stalking and Intimate Partner Femicide." *Homicide Studies* 3(4) (November 1999): 300-316, NCJ 179872.
http://www.ncjrs.gov/App/Publications/abstract.aspx?ID=179872

157. McFarlane, J., and A. Malecha. "Sexual Assault Among Intimates: Frequency, Consequences and Treatments." Final report for National Institute of Justice, grant number 2002-WG-BX-0003. Washington, DC: U.S. Department of Justice, National Institute of Justice, October 2005, NCJ 211678.
http://www.ncjrs.gov/App/Publications/abstract.aspx?ID=232957

158. Meehan, J., A. Holtzworth-Munroe, and K. Herron. "Maritally Violent Men"s Heart Rate Reactivity to Marital Interactions: A Failure to Replicate the Gottman et al. (1995) Typology." *Journal of Family Psychology* 15(3) (2001): 394-424.

159. Miller, N. "Queens County, New York, Arrest Policies Project: A Process Evaluation." Final report for National Institute of Justice, grant number 98-WE-VX-0012. Washington, DC: U.S. Department of Justice, National Institute of Justice, February 8, 2000, NCJ 201886.
http://www.ncjrs.gov/App/Publications/abstract.aspx?ID=201886

160. Miller, N. "Stalking Laws and Implementation Practices: A National Review for Policymakers and Practitioners." Final report for National Institute of Justice, grant number 97-WT-VX-0007. Washington, DC: U.S. Department of Justice, National Institute of Justice, October 2001, NCJ 197066.
http://www.ncjrs.gov/App/Publications/abstract.aspx?ID=197066

161. Miller, N. "What Does Research and Evaluation Say About Domestic Violence Laws? A Compendium of Justice System Laws and Related Research Assessments." Alexandria, VA: Institute for Law and Justice, December 2005, available online at
http://www.ilj.org/publications/dv/DomesticViolenceLegislationEvaluation.pdf.

162. Miller, S., and M. Meloy. "Women"s Use of Force: Voices of Women Arrested for Domestic Violence." *Violence Against Women* 12(1) (January 2006): 89-115, NCJ 212762.
http://www.ncjrs.gov/App/Publications/abstract.aspx?ID=234245

163. Murphy, C., P. Musser, and K. Maton. "Coordinated Community Intervention for Domestic Abusers: Intervention System Involvement and Criminal Recidivism." *Journal of Family Violence* 13(3) (September 1998): 263-284, NCJ 175131.
http://www.ncjrs.gov/App/Publications/abstract.aspx?ID=175131

164. Newmark, L., M. Rempel, K. Diffily, and K. Kane. "Specialized Felony Domestic Violence Court: Lessons on Implementation and Impacts from the Kings County Experience." Final report for National Institute of Justice, grant number 97-WT-VX-0005. Washington, DC: U.S. Department of Justice, National Institute of Justice, October 2001 (NCJ 191861) and 2004 (NCJ 199723). http://www.ncjrs.gov/App/Publications/abstract.aspx?ID=191861 and http://www.ncjrs.gov/App/Publications/abstract.aspx?ID=199723

165. New York State Division of Criminal Justice Services. "Family Protection and Domestic Violence Intervention Act of 1994: Evaluation of the Mandatory Arrest Provisions, Final Report." Supported in part by grant number 97-WE-VX-0128 from Violence Against Women Grants Office, Office of Justice Programs, U.S. Department of Justice. Albany, NY: Division of Criminal Justice Services, New York State Office for the Prevention of Domestic Violence, January 2001.

166. Niemi-Kiesiläinen, J. "The Deterrent Effect of Arrest in Domestic Violence: Differentiating Between Victim and Perpetrator Response." *Hastings Women's Law Journal* 12(2) (2001): 283-305.

167. Norwood, W., E. Jouriles, R. McDonald, and P. Swank. "Domestic Violence and Deviant Behavior." Final report for National Institute of Justice, grant number 98-WT-VX-0005.

Washington, DC: U.S. Department of Justice, National Institute of Justice, 2004, NCJ 199713.
http://www.ncjrs.gov/App/Publications/abstract.aspx?ID=199713

168. O'Farrell, T., W. Fals-Stewart, M. Murphy, and C. Murphy. "Partner Violence Before and After Individually Based Alcoholism Treatment for Male Alcoholic Patients." *Journal of Consulting & Clinical Psychology* 71(1) (February 2003): 92-102.

169. Office of the Commissioner of Probation. *Over 8,500 Domestic Restraining Orders Filed Since September in Massachusetts.* Boston, MA: Office of the Commissioner of Probation, November 1992.

170. Olson, L., C. Crandall, and D. Broudy. "Getting Away With Murder: A Report of the New Mexico Female Intimate Partner Violence Death Review Team." Albuquerque, NM: Center for Injury Prevention Research and Education, University of New Mexico School of Medicine, 1998.

171. Olson, D., and L. Stalans. "Violent Offenders on Probation: Profile, Sentence, and Outcome Differences Among Domestic Violence and Other Violent Probationers." *Violence Against Women* 7(10) (October 2001): 1164-1185, NCJ 192015.
http://www.ncjrs.gov/App/Publications/abstract.aspx?ID=192015

172. Orchowsky, S. "Evaluation of a Coordinated Community Response to Domestic Violence: The Alexandria Domestic Violence Intervention Project." Final report for National Institute for Justice, grant number 95-WT-NX-0004. Washington, DC: U.S. Department of Justice, National Institute of Justice, September 1999, NCJ 179974.
http://www.ncjrs.gov/App/Publications/abstract.aspx?ID=179974

173. Ostrom, B., and N. Kauder. *Examining the Work of State Courts, 1998: A National Perspective From the Court Statistics Project.* Williamsburg, VA: National Center for State Courts, 1999.

174. Pate, A., E. Hamilton, and S. Annan. "Metro-Dade Spouse Abuse Replication Project Technical Report." Final report for National Institute of Justice, grant number 87-IJ-CX-K003. Washington, DC: U.S. Department of Justice, National Institute of Justice, 1991, NCJ 139734.
http://www.ncjrs.gov/App/Publications/abstract.aspx?ID=139734

175. Pattavina, A., D. Hirschel, E. Buzawa, D. Faggiani, and H. Bentley. "Comparison of the Police Response to Heterosexual Versus Same-Sex Intimate Partner Violence." *Violence Against Women* 13(4) (April 2007): 374-394, NCJ 218287.
http://www.ncjrs.gov/App/Publications/abstract.aspx?ID=239986

176. Paulkossi, L. "Surveillance for Homicide Among Intimate Partners: United States, 1991-1998." *Morbidity and Mortality Weekly Surveillance Summaries* 5 (October 2001): 1-16.

177. Pence, E., and S. Dasgupta. "Re-Examining „Battering": Are All Acts of Violence Against Intimate Partners the Same?" Final report to Office on Violence Against Women, U.S. Department of Justice, grant number 1998-WR-VX-K001. Duluth, MN: Praxis International, June 2006.

178. Pennel, S., C. Burke, and D. Mulmat. "Violence Against Women in San Diego." Final report for National Institute of Justice, grant number 97-IJ-CX-0007. Washington, DC: U.S. Department of Justice, National Institute of Justice, March 2000, NCJ 191838.
http://www.ncjrs.gov/App/Publications/abstract.aspx?ID=191838

179. Peterson, R., and J. Dixon. "Examining Prosecutorial Discretion in Domestic Violence Cases." Paper presented at the American Society of Criminology, Toronto, Ontario, Canada, November 2005.

180. Peterson, W., and S. Thunberg. "Domestic Violence Court: Evaluation Report for the San Diego County Domestic Violence Courts." Report submitted by San Diego Superior Court to State Justice Institute, grant number SJI-98-N-271. San Diego, CA: San Diego Superior Court, September 2000, NCJ 187846.
http://www.ncjrs.gov/App/Publications/abstract.aspx?ID=187846

181. Pirog-Good, M., and J. Stets. "Programs for Abusers: Who Drops Out and What Can Be Done?" *Response to the Victimization of Women & Children* 9(2) (1986): 17-19.

182. Ptacek, J. *Battered Women in the Courtroom: The Power of Judicial Responses.* Northeastern Series on Gender, Crime, and Law. Boston, MA: Northeastern University Press, 1999, NCJ 183008.
http://www.ncjrs.gov/App/Publications/abstract.aspx?ID=183008

183. Puffett, N., and C. Gavin. "Predictors of Program Outcome and Recidivism at the Bronx Misdemeanor Domestic Violence Court." Funded by grants from Violence Against Women Office and New York State Office of Court Administration. New York, NY: Center for Court Innovation, April 2004, available online at
http://www.courtinnovation.org/ uploads/documents/predictorsbronxdv.pdf.

184. Raiford, L. "Report of the New York City Police Department Domestic Violence Unit." New York, NY: New York City Police Department, Domestic Violence Unit, March 2002, cited in A. Klein, *The Criminal Justice Response to Domestic Violence.* Belmont, CA: Wadsworth/Thomson, 2004: 90.

185. Rempel, M., M. Labriola, and R. Davis. "Does Judicial Monitoring Deter Domestic Violence Recidivism? Results of a Quasi-Experimental Comparison in the Bronx." *Violence Against Women* 14(2) (February 2008): 185-207, available online at
http://vaw.sagepub.com/cgi/content/abstract/14/2/185.

186. Rennison, C., and S. Welchans. *Intimate Partner Violence.* Special Report. Washington, DC: U.S. Department of Justice, Bureau of Justice Statistics, May 2000, NCJ 178247.
http://www.ncjrs.gov/App/Publications/abstract.aspx?ID=178247

187. Rigakos, G. "Situational Determinants of Police Responses to Civil and Criminal Injunctions for Battered Women." *Violence Against Women* 3(2) (April 1997): 204-216, available online at http://vaw.sagepub.com/cgi/content/abstract/3/2/204.

188. Roehl, J. "Police Use of Domestic Violence Information Systems." Final report for National Institute of Justice, grant number 95-IJ-CX-0097. Washington, DC: U.S. Department of

Justice, National Institute of Justice, February 1997, NCJ 182435.
http://www.ncjrs.gov/App/Publications/abstract.aspx?ID=182435

189. Roehl, J., and K. Guertin. "Intimate Partner Violence: The Current Use of Risk Assessments in Sentencing Offenders." *Justice System Journal* 21(2) (2000): 171-198, NCJ 183443.
http://www.ncjrs.gov/App/Publications/abstract.aspx?ID=183443

190. Roehl, J., C. O'Sullivan, D. Webster, and J. Campbell. "Intimate Partner Violence Risk Assessment Validation Study: The RAVE Study — Practitioner Summary and Recommendations: Validation of Tools for Assessing Risk From Violent Intimate Partners." Final report for National Institute of Justice, grant number 2000-WT-VX-0011. Washington, DC: U.S. Department of Justice, National Institute of Justice, May 2005, NCJ 209732.
http://www.ncjrs.gov/App/Publications/abstract.aspx?ID=209732

191. Rothman, E., D. Hemenway, M. Miller, and D. Azrel. "Batterers" Use of Guns to Threaten Intimate Partners." *Journal of the American Medical Women's Association* 60(1) (Winter 2004): 62-67.

192. Salomon, A., E. Bassuk, A. Browne, S. Bassuk, R. Dawson, and N. Huntington. "Secondary Data Analysis on the Etiology, Course, and Consequences of Intimate Partner Violence Against Extremely Poor Women." Final report for National Institute of Justice, grant number 98-WT-VX-0012. Washington, DC: U.S. Department of Justice, National Institute of Justice, 2004, NCJ 199714.
http://www.ncjrs.gov/App/Publications/abstract.aspx?ID=199714

193. Saunders, D. "Typology of Men Who Batter: Three Types Derived From Cluster Analysis." *American Journal of Orthopsychiatry* 62(2) (April 1992): 264-275, NCJ 139828.
http://www.ncjrs.gov/App/Publications/abstract.aspx?ID=139828

194. Saunders, D., and J. Parker. "Legal Sanctions and Treatment Follow-Through Among Men Who Batter: A Multivariate Analysis." *Social Work Research and Abstracts* 25(3) (1989): 21-29.

195. Smith, A. "Domestic Violence Laws: The Voices of Battered Women." *Violence and Victims* 16(1) (February 2001): 91-111, NCJ 187744.
http://www.ncjrs.gov/App/Publications/abstract.aspx?ID=187744

196. Smith, B., R. Davis, L. Nickles, and H. Davies. "Evaluation of Efforts to Implement No-Drop Policies: Two Central Values in Conflict." Final report for National Institute of Justice, grant number 98-WT-VX-0029. Washington, DC: U.S. Department of Justice, National Institute of Justice, March 2001, NCJ 187772.
http://www.ncjrs.gov/App/Publications/abstract.aspx?ID=187772

197. Smithey, M., S. Green, and A. Giacomazzi. "Collaborative Effort and the Effectiveness of Law Enforcement Training Toward Resolving Domestic Violence." Final report for National Institute of Justice, grant number 97-WE-VX-0131. Washington, DC: U.S. Department of Justice, National Institute of Justice, November 2000, NCJ 191840.
http://www.ncjrs.gov/App/Publications/abstract.aspx?ID=191840

198. Stark, E. *Coercive Control: How Men Entrap Women in Personal Life.* New York: Oxford University Press, 2007.

199. Starr, K., M. Hobart, and J. Fawcett. "Every Life Lost Is a Call for Change: Findings and Recommendations From the Washington State Domestic Violence Fatality Review." Seattle, WA: Washington State Coalition Against Domestic Violence, December 2004, available online at http://www.wscadv.org/pages.cfm?aId=9BF3F91C-C298-58F608C8E952508A52AD.

200. Steketee, M., L. Levey, and S. Keilitz. "Implementing an Integrated Domestic Violence Court: Systemic Change in the District of Columbia." Final report for State Justice Institute, grant number SJI-98-N-016. Williamsburg, VA: National Center for State Courts, and Alexandria, VA: State Justice Institute, June 30, 2000, NCJ 198516.
http://www.ncjrs.gov/App/Publications/abstract.aspx?ID=198516

201. Stith, S., K. Rosen, and E. McCollum. "Effectiveness of Couples Treatment for Spouse Abuse." *Journal of Marital and Family Therapy* 29(3) (2003): 407-426.

202. Straus, M., R. Gelles, and S. Steinmetz. *Behind Closed Doors: Violence in the American Family.* Garden City, NY: Doubleday, 1980, NCJ 148986.
http://www.ncjrs.gov/App/Publications/abstract.aspx?ID=148986

203. Stuart, G. "Improving Violence Intervention Outcomes Integrating Alcohol Treatment." *Journal of Interpersonal Violence* 20(4) (2005): 388-393.

204. Syers, M., and J. Edleson. "The Combined Effects of Coordinated Criminal Justice Intervention in Women Abuse." *Journal of Interpersonal Violence* 7(4) (December 1992): 490-502, NCJ 139788.
http://www.ncjrs.gov/App/Publications/abstract.aspx?ID=139788

205. Taylor, B., R. Davis, and C. Maxwell. "The Effects of a Group Batterer Treatment Program: A Randomized Experiment in Brooklyn." *Justice Quarterly* 18(1) (March 2001): 171-201, NCJ 187428.
http://www.ncjrs.gov/App/Publications/abstract.aspx?ID=187428

206. Thistlethwaite, A., J. Wooldredge, and D. Gibbs. "Severity of Dispositions and Domestic Violence Recidivism." *Crime and Delinquency* 44(3) (July 1998): 388-398, NCJ 173565.
http://www.ncjrs.gov/App/Publications/abstract.aspx?ID=173565

207. Tjaden, P., and N. Thoennes. *Stalking in America: Findings From the National Violence Against Women Survey.* Research in Brief. Washington, DC: U.S. Department of Justice, National Institute of Justice, grant number 93-IJ-CX-0012, April 1998, NCJ 169592.
http://www.ncjrs.gov/App/Publications/abstract.aspx?ID=169592

208. Tjaden, P., and N. Thoennes. *Prevalence, Incidence, and Consequences of Violence Against Women: Findings From the National Violence Against Women Survey.* Research in Brief. Washington, DC, and Atlanta, GA: U.S. Department of Justice, National Institute of Justice, and Centers for Disease Control and Prevention, grant number 93-IJ-CX-0012, November 1998, NCJ 172837.

http://www.ncjrs.gov/App/Publications/abstract.aspx?ID=172837

209. Tjaden, P., and N. Thoennes. "Extent, Nature, and Consequences of Intimate Partner Violence: Findings From the National Violence Against Women Survey." Final report for National Institute of Justice, grant number 93-IJ-CX-0012. Washington, DC: U.S. Department of Justice, National Institute of Justice, July 2000, NCJ 181867.
http://www.ncjrs.gov/App/Publications/abstract.aspx?ID=181867

210. Tjaden, P., and N. Thoennes. "Stalking: Its Role in Serious Domestic Violence Cases." Final report for National Institute of Justice, grant number 97-WT-VX-0002. Washington, DC: U.S. Department of Justice, National Institute of Justice, January 2001, NCJ 187346.
http://www.ncjrs.gov/App/Publications/abstract.aspx?ID=187346

211. Tolman, R., and A. Weisz. "Coordinated Community Intervention for Domestic Violence: The Effects of Arrest and Prosecution on Recidivism of Woman Abuse Perpetrators." Bureau of Justice Assistance and Illinois Criminal Justice Information Authority, grant number 90-DB-CX-0017. *Crime and Delinquency* 41(4) (October 1995): 481-495, NCJ 157475.
http://www.ncjrs.gov/App/Publications/abstract.aspx?ID=157475

212. Torres, S., and H. Han. "Psychological Distress in Non-Hispanic White and Hispanic Abused Women." *Archives of Psychiatric Nursing* 14(1) (February 2000): 19-29.

213. Townsend, M., D. Hunt, S. Kuck, and C. Baxter. "Law Enforcement Response to Domestic Violence Calls for Service." Final report for National Institute of Justice, grant number 99-C-008. Washington, DC: U.S. Department of Justice, National Institute of Justice, February 2005, NCJ 215915.
http://www.ncjrs.gov/App/Publications/abstract.aspx?ID=237504

214. U.S. Commission on Civil Rights. *Under the Rule of Thumb: Battered Women and the Administration of Justice*, Washington DC: U.S. Department of Justice, 1982, NCJ 082752.
http://www.ncjrs.gov/App/Publications/abstract.aspx?ID=82752

215. Ursel, J., and S. Brickey. "The Potential of Legal Reform Reconsidered: An Examination of Manitoba"s Zero-Tolerance Policy on Family Violence." In T. O"Reilly-Fleming, ed., *Post-Critical Criminology*. Scarborough, Ontario, Canada: Prentice-Hall, 1996: 6-77.

216. Ventura, L., and G. Davis. "Domestic Violence: Court Case Conviction and Recidivism." *Violence Against Women* 11(2) (February 2005): 255-277, NCJ 208869.
http://www.ncjrs.gov/App/Publications/abstract.aspx?ID=208869

217. Vigdor, E., and J. Mercy. "Do Laws Restricting Access to Firearms by Domestic Violence Offenders Prevent Intimate Partner Homicide?" *Evaluation Review* 30(3) (June 2006): 313-346.

218. Websdale, N., M. Sheeran, and B. Johnson. "Reviewing Domestic Violence Fatalities: Summarizing National Developments." Final report to Office on Violence Against Women, Office of Justice Programs, U.S. Department of Justice, grant 98-WT-VX-K001, and Minnesota Center Against Violence and Abuse, University of Minnesota. Violence Against

Women Online Resources, 1998, available online at
http://www.vaw.umn.edu/documents/fatality/fatality.html.

219. Weiss, H., B. Lawrence, and T. Miller. (2004). "Pregnancy-Associated Assault Hospitalizations: Prevalence and Risk of Hospitalized Assaults Against Women During Pregnancy." Final report for National Institute of Justice, grant number 1998-WT-VX-0016, Washington, DC: U.S. Department of Justice, National Institute of Justice, 2004, NCJ 199706.
http://www.ncjrs.gov/App/Publications/abstract.aspx?ID=199706

220. Weisz, A., D. Canales-Portalatin, and N. Nahan. "Evaluation of Victim Advocacy Within a Team Approach." Final report for National Institute for Justice, grant number 97-WT-VX-0006. Washington, DC: U.S. Department of Justice, National Institute of Justice, January 2001, NCJ 187107.
http://www.ncjrs.gov/App/Publications/abstract.aspx?ID=187107

221. Wekerle, C., and A. Wall. *The Violence and Addiction Equation: Theoretical and Clinical Issues in Substance Abuse and Relationship Violence.* New York, NY: Brunner-Routledge, 2002.

222. White, J., and P. Smith. "A Longitudinal Perspective on Physical and Sexual Intimate Partner Violence Against Women." Final report for National Institute of Justice, grant number 98-WT-VX-0010. Washington, DC: U.S. Department of Justice, National Institute of Justice, 2004, NCJ 199708.
http://www.ncjrs.gov/App/Publications/abstract.aspx?ID=199708

223. Williams, K., and A.-M. Houghton. "Assessing the Risk of Domestic Violence Reoffending: A Validation Study." *Law and Human Behavior* 28(4) (August 2004): 437-455.

224. Wilson, D., and A. Klein. "A Longitudinal Study of a Cohort of Batterers Arraigned in a Massachusetts District Court 1995 to 2004." Final report for National Institute of Justice, grant number 2004-WB-GX-0011. Washington, DC: U.S. Department of Justice, National Institute of Justice, May 2006, NCJ 215346.
http://www.ncjrs.gov/App/Publications/abstract.aspx?ID=236929

225. Wooldredge, J. "Convicting and Incarcerating Felony Offenders of Intimate Assault and the Odds of New Assault Charges." *Journal of Criminal Justice* 35(4) (July/August 2007): 379-389, NCJ 219877.
http://www.ncjrs.gov/App/Publications/abstract.aspx?ID=241675

226. Wooldredge, J., and A. Thistlethwaite. "Court Dispositions and Rearrest for Intimate Assault." *Crime and Delinquency* 51(1) (January 2005): 75-102, NCJ 208203.
http://www.ncjrs.gov/App/Publications/abstract.aspx?ID=208203

227. Worden, A. "Models of Community Coordination in Partner Violence Cases: A Multi-Site Comparative Analysis." Final report for National Institute of Justice, grant number 95-WT-NX-0006. Washington, DC: U.S. Department of Justice, National Institute of Justice, February 2001, NCJ 187351.
http://www.ncjrs.gov/App/Publications/abstract.aspx?ID=187351

228. Wordes, M. "Creating a Structured Decision-Making Model for Police Intervention in Intimate Partner Violence." Final report for National Institute of Justice, grant number 96-IJ-CX-0098. Washington, DC: U.S. Department of Justice, National Institute of Justice, February 2000, NCJ 182781.
http://www.ncjrs.gov/App/Publications/abstract.aspx?ID=182781

JUNE 09

NCJ 225722

www.ingramcontent.com/pod-product-compliance
Lightning Source LLC
Chambersburg PA
CBHW081139170526
45165CB00008B/2726